EVALUATION TOOLKIT LIBRARY
ETS   Research Division
Princeton, New Jersey

EVALUATION TOOLKIT LIBRARY
ETS   Research Division
Princeton, New Jersey

APPLICATIONS OF CASE STUDY RESEARCH

Second Edition

Applied Social Research Methods Series
Volume 34

APPLIED SOCIAL RESEARCH METHODS SERIES

Series Editors

LEONARD BICKMAN, Peabody College, Vanderbilt University, Nashville
DEBRA J. ROG, Vanderbilt University, Washington, DC

Other volumes in this series are listed at the back of the book

APPLICATIONS OF CASE STUDY RESEARCH

Second Edition

Robert K. Yin

Applied Social Research Methods Series
Volume 34

SAGE Publications
International Educational and Professional Publisher
Thousand Oaks ▪ London ▪ New Delhi

Copyright © 2003 by Sage Publications, Inc.

All rights reserved. No part of this book may be reproduced or utilized in any form or by any means, electronic or mechanical, including photocopying, recording, or by any information storage and retrieval system, without permission in writing from the publisher.

For information:

Sage Publications, Inc.
2455 Teller Road
Thousand Oaks, California 91320
E-mail: order@sagepub.com

Sage Publications Ltd.
6 Bonhill Street
London EC2A 4PU
United Kingdom

Sage Publications India Pvt. Ltd.
B-42 Panchsheel Enclave
Post Box 4109
New Delhi 110 017 India

Printed in the United States of America

Library of Congress Cataloging-in-Publication Data

Yin, Robert K.
Applications of case study research / Robert K. Yin.— 2nd ed.
    p. cm. — (Applied social research methods series ; v. 34)
Includes bibliographical references and index. ISBN 0-7619-2550-3
(cloth : acid-free paper) —
ISBN 0-7619-2551-1 (paper : acid-free paper)
    1. Social sciences—Methodology. 2. Case method. I. Title. II. Series.
H61 .Y56 2003
300'.7'22—dc21
                    2002152714

This book is printed on acid-free paper.

02 03 04 05 10 9 8 7 6 5 4 3 2 1

Production Editor:	Sanford Robinson
Editorial Assistant:	Karen Wiley
Typesetter:	C&M Digitals (P) Ltd.
Indexer:	Molly Hall

Contents

Preface and Acknowledgments

You (a seasoned investigator or a budding researchers) are likely to value this book for either of (and possibly only) two reasons: (1) You already are committed to doing case studies and are seeking additional information to improve your craft, or (2) you still have been unconvinced about doing case studies and hope that having access to specific, concrete examples will provide more information to make up your mind. To address either situation, the book presents numerous completed case studies on a broad variety of topics. To cover this breadth and to make the case studies more readable, many have been condensed or abbreviated from their original form. However, all retain their essential technical features, to demonstrate how case study research has been successfully conducted.

The book complements a companion textbook on *Case Study Research: Design and Methods*, first published in 1989 (the third edition also was published in 2003). The companion text provides operational guidance about case studies and cites a large number of well-known if not famous case studies that are available in journals and books. However, that text does not contain any actual case studies. In contrast, this book discusses more than a dozen case studies in one fashion or another. Furthermore, the 10 chapters of this book contain almost an entirely new set of contemporary case studies compared to those in the book's 1993 edition, with the material in only one chapter (Chapter 1) overlapping the two previous editions.

As in this book's 1993 edition, the entire array of case study applications comes from the portfolio of projects at COSMOS Corporation, an applied social research think tank. Since its inception in 1980, COSMOS has been avidly practicing case study (as well as other types of) research. The case study research portion of the portfolio over the last decade has covered many different subjects, and from these the present collection has been selected. Most important, the selected case studies all put into practice sound principles of case study research, reflecting the entire range of processes and procedures from research design to research reporting. These case study applications therefore identify and suggest solutions to problems commonly encountered when doing case studies.

By way of acknowledgment, the work in this book reflects the stimulation and continued encouragement and support of many key persons. The editors of this Sage Publications series on Applied Social Research Methods—Professor Leonard Bickman and Dr. Debra Rog—have been strong supporters from the very beginning. They are to be thanked for their understanding of the place of case study research in the broader array of social science methods and for their incessant demands for more and better manuscripts on the topic. In addition, federal agencies and their project officers who have sponsored and continue to support a stream of projects using case studies (many cited in the chapters of this book) are to be acknowledged and thanked.

Research colleagues also have stimulated the development of new ideas. Earlier, the collegial relationships were related to the teaching of courses at The Massachusetts Institute of Technology and the American University (Washington, D.C.) or to summer institutes organized by the Aarhus School of Business (University of Aarhus) in Denmark.

More recently, many research colleagues from a variety of universities and research organizations have participated in case study workshops as part of COSMOS's projects. Whether posed at these workshops or in related e-mails, your continued questions about how to use case studies to clarify specific research issues, or about the particular implications of the method for the research topics you have been investigating, often have led serendipitously to new insights about case study research.

Similarly, staff and consultants at COSMOS have struggled with numerous case studies and case study research projects, creating an exciting learning environment that seems to evolve endlessly and to reach continually into as yet unexplored vistas, despite the passage of over two decades. To prepare the current manuscript, three people at COSMOS also were especially helpful: Dawn Kim, who helped to track down and recall the relevant circumstances in which individual case studies had been conducted; Bob Johnson, for his continued creative graphics; and Tonia Quintanilla, for fixing and recasting the text and especially the figures and tables to meet Sage publication guidelines.

Finally, the book is dedicated as before to Karen, my spouse, friend, and mother of our son Andrew. She has continually nurtured great expectations for both of us, and her love has endured the many hours absorbed by the writing, travel, and presentations associated with the ideas in this book. Andrew is now 10 years old and, like Karen, also has suffered repeated references to case study research. Thanks to both of you for your support, patience, and love.

Introduction

Case study research continues to be an essential form of social science inquiry. The method is appropriate when investigators either desire or are forced by circumstances (a) to define research topics broadly and not narrowly, (b) to cover contextual or complex multivariate conditions and not just isolated variables, and (c) to rely on multiple and not singular sources of evidence.

The method should be one of several that a social scientist or team of social scientists is capable of using. Other methods include doing surveys, designing and conducting experiments, using quantitative models to analyze archival records, dealing with historical documents (e.g., historiography), and doing qualitative research (e.g., ethnography). Depending upon the situation, case studies may be conducted alone or in combination with these other methods, as all have complementary strengths and weaknesses.

Numerous researchers and students continue to want or need to do case studies on such diverse topics as business and organizational issues, education, child and youth development, family studies, international affairs, technology development, and research on social problems. In addition, case studies have long been one of the most common methods of conducting research for use in public policy and in business and public administration.

During the latter decades of the 20th century, case studies of specific programs, projects, initiatives, or sites also became an integral part of evaluation research. In an evaluative context, the case studies have generally been used to document and analyze implementation processes. Case studies, therefore, have been associated with *process* evaluations. However, as demonstrated by some of the case studies in this book, the method also has been and can be used to document and analyze the *outcomes* of public or privately supported interventions, such as the programs sponsored by federal agencies or the initiatives supported by private foundations. At the same time, none of these uses of case study research pertains to their use as a teaching tool, which is not the subject of this book.

Yet, among nearly all social science research methods, case study research has received perhaps the least attention and guidance. The methodological literature covers the topic infrequently. Academic courses about designing and doing research case studies are rare. Although many textbooks are devoted to a closely related method—qualitative research—only a few texts deal directly with the case study method. Moreover, existing modes of information dissemination do not provide the forums to develop or convey such guidance. For instance, no journal of case study research exists, and no journal focuses exclusively on case study research methods.

Similarly, the most common textbooks on social science methods in general and evaluation research methods in particular still give only passing mention to the case study method, if it is covered at all. You also should beware that when the topic is only briefly discussed, the discussion may be misleading—typically confusing case study research with qualitative research or with unacceptable quasi-experimental designs. Suffice it to say that, apart from either of these other two types of research, case study research has its own method and rationale but still lacks adequate recognition.

Applications of Case Study Research tries to fill a little of this void. Offered are a variety of examples of practical and contemporary applications of case study research methods. All the applications come from longer, completed investigations designed or conducted by the author. Most of the applications appear as separate chapters.[1] The applications demonstrate specific techniques or principles that are integral to the case study method and that have been discussed in a companion textbook, *Case Study Research: Design and Methods* (Yin, 2003). By having access to these specific applications, seasoned investigators and students alike should be better able to emulate case study research techniques and principles in their own research.

DIVERSITY OF APPLICATIONS IN THIS BOOK

In any situation, the nature of examples or applications is that they are specific. As a result, interest in any one of them is likely to be narrow. Some applications will be directly relevant to research projects at hand or being contemplated, but other applications will seem to be part of some alien world with an unfriendly technical vocabulary.

Given this circumstance, two strategies were used in composing this book, to make it as attractive and useful to as broad a research audience as possible. First, the book contains applications on a diverse array of topics, in the hope that every reader will find at least one application directly relevant to his or her ongoing case study research interests. Second, the applications have been organized to cover different methodological issues. Let's talk about the diversity first.

The book has more examples of case studies on efforts taking place in local communities than any other type, because these have most commonly been topics of case study inquiry in the public arena. The efforts cover a broad range of local services and local initiatives, such as education (Chapters 1 and 3), law enforcement (Chapter 7), public health (Chapter 8), substance abuse prevention (Chapter 5), local economic development (Chapter 1), job training (Chapter 1), and neighborhood organizations (Chapter 2). Still at the local level, community partnerships and interorganizational partnerships of one sort or another (Chapters 1 and 5) also have been topics of interest in many fields. Finally, the peculiar problem of understanding how urban service innovations become routinized or sustained over long periods of time also is the topic of one case study (Chapter 1).

The book also recognizes interest in conducting research on universities by covering two administrative issues universally important to all such institutions—the computerization of technical functions (Chapter 4) and the production of high volumes of research proposals (Chapter 9).

Moving away from the public and nonprofit sector, the book also has two applications covering the workings of manufacturing firms (Chapters 6 and 8) and one on high-technology and industrial parks (Chapter 1). There also is one case study on a common but poorly understood dissemination or diffusion process, whereby good ideas in natural hazards research are eventually put into both commercial and public practice (Chapter 1).

Missing from the collection is another common brand of case studies: case studies of individual persons. This type of case study already appears to be represented well in the clinical literature (e.g., clinical psychology, psychiatry, and social work), in biographies and oral histories of famous people, and in related fields such as criminology and its case studies of archetypal criminal offenders. The absence of such case studies in this volume does not mean that they are any less important, but the greater challenge over the years seems to have been on doing case studies to investigate institutional or organizational phenomena, which are therefore the genre of topics represented in this book.

METHODOLOGICAL TOPICS COVERED AND THE ORGANIZATION OF THIS BOOK

Methodological Topics

A second strategy used to make this book attractive and useful to as broad a research audience as possible relates to methodological issues: The selected cases deliberately cover the important methodological issues encountered in doing case study research. The book's 10 chapters have been organized into four parts, each covering a broadly significant methodological category for designing or doing case study research:

- *Part I:* The role of theory in doing case studies, containing examples of exploratory, descriptive, and explanatory case studies (Chapter 1)
- *Part II:* Examples of descriptive case studies (Chapters 2 and 3)
- *Part III:* Examples of explanatory case studies (Chapters 4 through 7)
- *Part IV:* Examples of cross-case or multiple-case studies (Chapters 8 through 10)

The four parts are intended to direct your attention to the most commonly used categories of case studies so that, for instance, if you want to do a descriptive case study, you should turn first to the examples in Parts I and II.

Of these four parts, the first deviates from being a type of case study and deserves further explanation. The role of theory in doing case studies may possibly be your single most important aid in doing case study research. Theory is not only helpful in designing a case study but also becomes the vehicle for generalizing a case study's results. This critical role of theory has been integral to the development of sound case studies, both single- and multiple-case. Part I therefore shows how to integrate theoretical concerns into exploratory case studies, descriptive case studies, or explanatory case studies. Part I also shows how theory can even enter the picture during the case selection process. You should know that if no other lesson is learned from this book, an understanding of the use of theory and an appreciation for the examples in Part I will go a long way to designing implementable, useful, and generalizable case studies.

Conversely, none of the four parts or chapter headings explicitly points to a burgeoning application of case studies: their use in doing *evaluation* research. However, the case studies in three chapters (5, 7, and 8) contain case studies that were done as part of larger evaluation projects at COSMOS. If you are mainly interested in seeing how case study research has been applied to contemporary evaluations, you can turn immediately to these three chapters.[2]

To guide you at a more detailed level, every chapter is introduced with a brief description covering the methodological highlights of the case study and background about its subject matter. Strewn throughout the book are a series of 21 boxes, each covering a key methodological concept or term used in that chapter, so you can more readily "apprentice" with the text. Furthermore, each box contains a brief cross-reference to the companion textbook, *Case Study Research: Design and Methods* (2003), where you can find even more information about the particular concept or term.

Overall, the goal has been to assemble a collection of individual case studies that covers the most commonly encountered methodological procedures in doing case study research, in addition to covering a diversity of topics. Table A.1 presents a comprehensive crosswalk of the methodological topics, referencing again the sections in the companion textbook. The crosswalk covers both the text and the 21 boxes on a chapter-by-chapter basis. Reading across the rows identifies the chapters in this book that contain applications for a particular methodological concept or term; reading down the columns refers you to additional methodological material covered by the companion textbook.

Organization of this Book

The following is a brief overview of the material in each chapter.

Part I: Theory. Chapter 1 shows how reliance on theoretical concepts remains one of the most important strategies for completing successful case studies, whether exploratory, descriptive, or explanatory. Thus, Part I covers the development of preliminary concepts at the outset of a case study, placing it within an appropriate research literature; defining the unit of analysis; identifying criteria for selecting and screening potential cases; and suggesting variables of interest. These steps are illustrated in five different case studies:

- How innovations in urban services become routinized
- Linking job training and economic development at the local level
- How to attract high-tech firms to research parks
- How and why research findings get into practical use
- Categorical versus noncategorical education for students with disabilities

Part II: Descriptive Case Studies. Chapter 2 (neighborhood organizations) shows how descriptive case studies can be organized into a series of questions and answers. Chapter 3 (computers in schools) illustrates how descriptive cases can attend to chronological sequences as an organizing theme and also have embedded units of analysis, shown in vignettes.

Table A.1.

Crosswalk Between Topics Found in Two Case Study Books

TOPIC FOUND IN *Case Study Research*	CHAPTER IN *Case Study Applications*																			
	1 T	1 B	2 T	2 B	3 T	3 B	4 T	4 B	5 T	5 B	6 T	6 B	7 T	7 B	8 T	8 B	9 T	9 B	10 T	10 B
CHAPTER 1: INTRODUCTION																				
Comparing Case Studies with Other Research		2																		
Types of Case Studies:		1																		21
-Exploratory	◆																			
-Descriptive	◆		◆		◆										◆					
-Explanatory	◆						◆		◆		◆		◆		◆				◆	
Qualitative and Quantitative Evidence				7					◆		◆		◆		◆					
Case Study Evaluations											◆		◆	12	◆					
CHAPTER 2: DESIGNING CASE STUDIES																				
Unit of Analysis	◆														◆	15				
Role of Theory in Doing Case Studies	◆	5									◆						◆		◆	
Case Study Designs:		2																		
-Single-Case Designs			◆		◆		◆		◆		◆		◆							
-Multiple-Case Designs		4													◆	13	◆	17	◆	19
-Holistic Designs			◆				◆		◆		◆		◆		◆				◆	
-Embedded Units of Analysis					◆												◆			
Replication Logic For Generalizing From Case Studies									◆						◆		◆		◆	
CHAPTER 3: PREPARING FOR DATA COLLECTION																				
Training and Preparation For a Case Study						8														
Case Study Protocol			◆		◆	9														
Screening Case Study Nominations	◆	3													◆					
Pilot Case Studies	◆																			
CHAPTER 4: COLLECTING THE EVIDENCE																				
Multiple Sources of Evidence			◆		◆						◆	10, 11	◆				◆		◆	
Case Study Database			◆	6																
Chain of Evidence			◆																	
CHAPTER 5: ANALYZING CASE STUDY EVIDENCE																				
Relying on Theoretical Propositions	◆														◆					
Rival Explanations									◆				◆		◆	16				
Specific Techniques:																				
-Pattern Matching	◆														◆		◆		◆	
-Explanation building	◆								◆								◆	18	◆	
-Chronology					◆				◆		◆		◆						◆	
-Logic Models															◆	14	◆		◆	20
Cross-Case Synthesis															◆		◆		◆	
CHAPTER 6: REPORTING CASE STUDIES																				
Case Study Reports as Part of Larger, Multimethod Studies	◆												◆							
Case Identities:																				
-Real			◆		◆		◆				◆		◆		◆				◆	
-Anonymous									◆								◆			

KEY: ◆ = topic discussed in text (T) of cited chapter; numbers = boxes (B) found in cited chapter

Part III: Explanatory Case Studies. In Chapter 4 (university computer department), a potential causal path is embedded in an explanation. Explanatory cases can suggest important clues to cause-and-effect relationships, but not with the certainty of true experiments. The basic claim underlying each of the three cases in Chapter 5 (community partnerships for substance abuse prevention) is that a community formed a partnership to support activities critical to substance abuse prevention. The cases also show how the use of rival hypotheses can partially compensate for the absence of comparison cases. Chapter 6 (medium-sized manufacturing firms) uses multiple sources of evidence to show how a strategic planning process led to long-term transformation of an organization. Chapter 7 (local law enforcement) describes the outcomes from a local public sector innovation and whether external funding led to the innovative practice. The chapter also shows the importance of tracking chronological sequence of events to help interpret potency of rival explanation.

Part IV: Cross-Case Analyses. Chapter 8 (HIV/AIDS community planning) amasses findings from eight explanatory case studies, each assessing the provision of technical assistance to a community group. The design is based on a replication logic. Chapter 9 (university proposal processing) presents a case study explaining a sequence of events without having an intervention that is the subject of evaluation. The chapter also illustrates the use of quantitative and qualitative data. Chapter 10 (transforming firms) gives a traditional cross-case analysis of 14 individual case studies.

ON EMULATING THE SCIENTIFIC METHOD

Readers familiar with the previous edition of the companion text will know that its approach to case study research favors emulation of the scientific method. The method underlies all science and includes the following steps:

1. Posing explicit research questions
2. Developing a formal research design
3. Using theory and reviews of previous research to develop hypotheses and rival hypotheses
4. Collecting empirical data to test these hypotheses and rival hypotheses
5. Assembling a database—independent of any narrative report, interpretations, or conclusions—that can be inspected by third parties
6. Conducting quantitative or qualitative analyses (or both), depending upon the topic and research design

The present book continues this emulation of the scientific method. Such emulation is considered an essential way of improving the quality of case study research. However, because of this stance, some critics of this approach to case studies have mistaken the emulation as a claim that doing case studies in this manner is the same as doing science. You should know that no one yet has the evidence or argument to make this claim. My only claim is that case studies that are based on the philosophy of "normal" science and that use its procedures are likely to be of higher quality than case studies that do not. But doing case studies is not necessarily the same as doing science (just as doing social science is not necessarily the same as doing science), and the matter deserves clarification. I hope that you the readers will share in the clarification process.

NOTES

1. Chapter 1 actually covers five different case studies and Chapter 5 covers three. Each of the other chapters is limited to one single- or multiple-case study.

2. For more on this important use of case studies, see Robert K. Yin, "The Case Study Method as a Tool for Doing Evaluation," *Current Sociology,* Spring 1992, Volume 40, pp. 121-137 (a slightly expanded version appeared in the first edition of the present book).

PART I

Theory

1

The Role of Theory in Doing Case Studies

Reliance on theoretical concepts to guide the design and data collection for case studies remains one of the most important strategies for completing successful case studies. Such theoretical concepts can be useful in conducting exploratory, descriptive, or explanatory (causal) case studies.

The goal is to develop preliminary concepts at the outset of a case study. One purpose served by such concepts, as in any other empirical study, is to place the case study in an appropriate research literature, so that lessons from the case study will more likely advance knowledge and understanding of a given topic. A second purpose, possibly more important for case studies than for other types of research, is to help define the unit of analysis (what is the case?), to identify the criteria for selecting and screening potential candidates for the cases to be studied, and to suggest the relevant variables of interest and therefore data to be collected as part of the case study. Without guidance from the preliminary theoretical concepts, all these choices may be extremely difficult and hamper the development of a rigorous case study.

How theory was used in five different case studies is the subject of the present chapter. The topics of the case studies cover (1) organizing local services and routinizing innovations, (2) forming and maintaining interorganizational partnerships, (3) attracting high-tech firms to locate in research parks, (4) explanations for how and why research findings are eventually put into practice, and (5) initiatives in special education (the education of students with disabilities) undertaken by four states. To demonstrate the usefulness of theoretical concepts in doing case study research, the five different case studies include examples of exploratory, descriptive, and explanatory (causal) case studies.

AUTHOR'S NOTE: This chapter is an expanded and adapted version of a paper that first appeared in Huey-tsyh Chen and Peter H. Rossi (Eds.), *Using Theory to Improve Program and Policy Evaluations* (pp. 97-114, 1992), an imprint of Greenwood Publishing Group, Inc., Westport, Connecticut. Used with permission.

WHAT IS THE CASE STUDY METHOD?

The case study is the method of choice when the phenomenon under study is not readily distinguishable from its context. Such a phenomenon may be a *project* or *program* in an evaluation study. Sometimes, the definition of this project or program may be problematic, as in determining when the activity started or ended—an example of a complex interaction between a phenomenon and its (temporal) context. Other examples of such complex interactions abound, including varied situations such as those discussed in subsequent chapters of this book—for example, a community organization and its neighborhood, the implementation of personal computers in schools, and a manufacturing firm and its marketplace (see Chapters 2, 3, and 6). All are situations warranting the use of case studies.

The inclusion of the context as a major part of a study, however, creates distinctive technical challenges. First, the richness of the context means that the ensuing study will likely have more variables than data points. Second, the richness means that the study cannot rely on a single data collection method but will likely need to use multiple sources of evidence. Third, even if all the relevant variables are quantitative, distinctive strategies will be needed for research design and for analysis. The development of rigorous techniques and strategies under these conditions—in comparison to the conditions faced by ethnography, history, quasi-experimentation, and surveys—has been the continuing quest in defining the case study method, as depicted in the companion to this book (Yin, 2003). Furthermore, a continuing priority is to consider case studies as a method not implying any preferred form of data collection.

WHAT IS THE ROLE OF THEORY IN DOING CASE STUDIES?

Revived interest in the role of theory in doing evaluations (Bickman, 1987; Chen, 1990; Chen & Rossi, 1989) has had a continued counterpart in the role of theory in designing and doing case studies. Critical examples include the importance of theory in explanatory (not just exploratory or descriptive) case studies (Yin, 1981a) as well as in multiple-case studies based on replication designs (Yin, 1981b). Overall, theory can be important to case studies in many ways, helping in the following areas:

BOX 1

Six Different Types of Case Studies

Theory and theoretical constructs are useful in all kinds of case studies, when case studies are used for research and not teaching or dissemination purposes.

For research, at least six kinds of case studies can be identified, based on a 2 × 3 matrix. First, case study research can be based on *single-* or *multiple-case* studies; second, whether single or multiple, the case study can be *exploratory, descriptive,* or *explanatory* (causal). The present chapter covers three of these six types.

In a nutshell, the 2 × 3 dimensions may be characterized as follows. A *single-case study* focuses on a single case only; *multiple-case studies,* however, include two or more cases within the same study. These multiple cases should be selected so that they replicate each other—either predicting similar results (literal replication) or contrasting results for predictable reasons (theoretical replication). An *exploratory* case study (whether based on single or multiple cases) is aimed at defining the questions and hypotheses of a subsequent study (not necessarily a case study) or at determining the feasibility of the desired research procedures. A *descriptive* case study presents a complete description of a phenomenon within its context. An *explanatory* case study presents data bearing on cause-effect relationships—explaining how events happened.

(For more information, see Yin, 2003, Chapter 1, sections on "Comparing Case Studies With Other Research Strategies in the Social Sciences" and "Variations in Case Studies.")

- Selecting the cases to be studied, whether following a single-case or multiple-case design (see Box 1)
- Specifying what is being explored when you are doing exploratory case studies
- Defining a complete and appropriate description when you are doing descriptive case studies
- Stipulating rival theories when you are doing explanatory case studies (see Box 1)
- Generalizing the results to other cases

From this perspective, the term *theory* covers more than causal theories. Rather, *theory* means the design of research steps according to some relationship to the literature, policy issues, or other substantive source.

Excluded would be considerations of access, convenience, logistics, or nonsubstantive issues. Good use of theory will help delimit a case study inquiry to its most effective design; theory is also essential for generalizing the subsequent results.

The purpose of this chapter is to provide specific illustrations of theory-based approaches to case study research and evaluations. Many of the classic illustrations have been cited elsewhere (Yin, 2003). The present chapter therefore is based on research done at COSMOS Corporation. Reported below are five important applications of theory to exploratory case studies, case study selection, two types of causal case studies, and descriptive case studies.

EXPLORATORY CASE STUDIES

The exploratory case study has perhaps given all of case study research its most notorious reputation. In this type of case study, fieldwork and data collection are undertaken prior to the final definition of study questions and hypotheses. Research may follow intuitive paths, often perceived by others as sloppy. However, the goal may justifiably be to discover theory by directly observing a social phenomenon in its raw form (Glaser & Strauss, 1967). Moreover, when the final study questions and hypotheses are settled, the final study may not necessarily be a case study but may assume some other form. The exploratory case study (see Box 2), therefore, has been considered a prelude to much social research, not just to other case studies (e.g., Ogawa & Malen, 1991; Yin, 1991).

An illustrative use of the exploratory case study occurred as part of a study on how innovations in urban services become routinized (Yin, 1981c; Yin, 1982; Yin et al., 1979). [Contemporary interest in this topic falls under the related concept of "sustainability."] Service agencies were experiencing difficulties in making such innovations survive beyond the adoption phase. This meant that an innovation might be put into place for a 2- or 3-year period, show promising results, but then stop being used. The policy relevance of the study was to determine how to avoid such an outcome.

The exploratory cases were conducted during the pilot test phase of the study, which involved 12 case studies and a telephone survey of 90 other sites. The study team spent an extended time in the exploratory phase and collected substantial data from seven sites (none of which were used in the final study). Such a high proportion of pilot to final case study sites (7 to 12) is exceptional, but the study team had important questions in need of answers.

BOX 2

Exploratory Case Studies

The exploratory phase of this study on innovations in urban services illustrates some of the challenges in doing exploratory case studies. Possibly the major problem with exploratory case studies arises when investigators wrongly use the data collected during the pilot phase as part of the ensuing case study. Whether a case study involves single or multiple cases, you should not permit such slippage from the exploratory (pilot) phase into the actual case study to occur.

An exploratory study should be taken at face value. You may have initially been uncertain about some major aspect of a real case study—the questions to be asked, the hypotheses of study, the data collection methods, the access to the data, or the data analytic methods—and therefore needed to investigate these issues. Once investigated, the pilot or exploratory phase should be considered completed. Now, you are ready to start the real study from scratch, with a complete research design, a whole new set of sources (sites) of information, and a fresh set of data. Furthermore, the pilot study also may have pointed to the need for a survey, experiment, or some method different from a case study.

(For more information, see Yin, 2003, Chapter 1, section on "Comparing Case Studies With Other Research Strategies in the Social Sciences," and Chapter 2, section on "Components of Research Designs.")

The Exploratory Issue: The Need to Create a Framework of Study

Only the broad features of the study design had been determined ahead of time. First, the study team was to select different types of innovations, covering different urban services. Second, the team would follow a retrospective design: The sites to be studied would be those in which routinization of an innovation was known to have occurred, so that the entire routinization process could be studied, even though the data had to be collected retrospectively. Third, the study team would emphasize actual behavioral events in the routinization processes, in contrast to an alternative methodology focusing on people's perceptions. However, within these broader themes, the specific design and data collection methods were unspecified. Thus, a pilot phase was designed to determine the innovations and services to be studied as well as the conceptual framework and operational measures to be used.

A key ingredient here was the use of a special pilot protocol that elaborated alternative features about the life cycle of an innovation. The study team understood that adoption-implementation-routinization potentially constituted the entire life cycle but had not developed specific hypotheses or measures to facilitate empirical study. In this sense, the protocol reflected the development of theory, not just methodological issues.

The study team modified this protocol after every pilot site study was completed. This iterative process forced the team to repeatedly address several questions: Had sufficient information been learned that an existing exploratory question could now be dropped? Had new problems emerged, requiring the framing of a new question? Did an existing question need to be modified? The team also deliberately varied the site visits. The first covered five different innovations, but not in much depth. Later site visits narrowed to one or two innovations, but with increasing data collection about each. Ultimately, hypotheses and the instrumentation for a full profile of an innovation's life history emerged.

Illustrative Results and Key Lessons

The pilot testing helped to identify six innovations in three urban services (law enforcement, education, and fire protection) that were ultimately studied at over 100 sites. However, the most important result of the pilot testing was the development of a conceptual framework and operational measures of a hypothesized routinization process. Measurable organizational events were identified as "cycles" or "passages," as illustrated in Table 1.1. Furthermore, certain cycles and passages were predicted to occur earlier in the routinization process, and others later. The framework made it possible for data to be collected and for the full study to proceed.

Another important result of the pilot testing was the finding that, whereas a single protocol could be used for the case studies, the study team had to design six separate questionnaires for the telephone survey, one for each type of innovation. For phone interviews, the terminology and events were sufficiently different that a generic set of questions could not be used. This discovery meant much unanticipated work on the part of the study team; in fact, the team resisted the finding throughout the pilot phase because of the known consequences in workload. However, no single questionnaire would work.

This experience with pilot testing shows how explicit explorations can elaborate key conceptual topics in some previously identified broad subject area. The use of a pilot protocol is strongly suggested as a tool for ensuring that the exploration is following some exploratory theory and that you are not merely wandering through the exploratory phase.

Table 1.1

Organizational Passages and Cycles Related to Routinization

Type or Operation of Resource	Passages	Sources
Budget	Innovation supports changes from soft to hard money	Survives annual budget cycles
Personnel: jobs	Functions become part of job descriptions or prerequisites	—
Incumbent turnover	—	Survives introduction of new personnel Survives promotion of key personnel
Training: prepractice	Skills become part of professional standards, professional school curriculum	—
In-service	—	Skills taught during many training cycles
Organizational governance	Innovative activity attains appropriate organizational status	Attains widespread use
Supply and maintenance	Supply and maintenance are provided by agency or on long-term (contract) basis	Survives equipment turnover

Source: Yin (1981c).

CASE SELECTION AND SCREENING: CRITERIA AND PROCEDURES

Selecting the case or cases to be studied is one of the most difficult steps in case study research (see Box 3). When you are uncertain about this process, the elaboration of theoretical issues related to the objectives of study can provide essential guidance.

The Research Issue: Linking Job Training and Economic Development at the Local Level

The difficulties of this process and how they were overcome are illustrated by a study of local job training and economic development efforts

---

BOX 3

Screening and Selecting Case Studies

The case study on the linkage between job training and local economic development called for an extensive (and intensive) procedure to screen the selected cases. Selecting the cases for a case study should not simply be a matter of finding the most convenient or accessible site from which you can collect data. The selection process needs to incorporate the specific reasons why you need a particular group of cases. For instance, you may need to have exemplary instances of the phenomenon being studied, or you may need a group that includes contrasting outcomes.

Whatever the reasons, the candidate cases should be screened beforehand, and you need to anticipate this as a step in your work plan. The screening process will involve collecting sufficient data to decide whether a case meets your preestablished criteria. The most desirable screening process will identify an array of candidate cases but without actually collecting so much data that the screening begins to emulate the conduct of the actual case studies. In other words, you need to be careful to avoid allowing the screening procedure to become too extensive or expensive.

(For more information, see Yin, 2003, Chapter 3, section on "Screening Case Study Nominations.")

(COSMOS, 1989). The example contains an extended selection process to help you develop a full appreciation of the potential steps. Many studies may not need to use all these steps or undertake them in such detail. However, the example provides a comprehensive template.

The study objective was to investigate how linkages between job training (for the hard-to-employ) and economic development efforts can produce distinctive outcomes. The potential advantages are that for the training participant, placement is more likely to occur in jobs in growing industries and occupations, resulting in more enduring job placements. Conversely, for employers, a larger pool of appropriately trained employees is created, thereby making recruitment easier. Without such linkages between job training and economic development, neither advantage is likely to be realized. Job training efforts alone can easily lead to placement in low-growth jobs for the hard-to-employ; economic development efforts alone can focus too heavily on employers' facilities and capital needs, overlooking their potential employment needs. A series of case studies was to examine these linkage situations and how these outcomes were produced.

However, although linkage was simple in concept, it was difficult to define operationally. What kinds of cases would be relevant?

Unit of Analysis

One challenge was to define the unit of analysis. The study team readily understood that this unit would not necessarily be a single organization or initiative. To study linkage, a joint organizational effort (between two or more organizations) or joint initiatives (job training and economic development) would likely be the unit of analysis. The identification of such joint efforts therefore became the first characteristic of the unit of analysis.

A more troubling characteristic involved the context for such joint efforts. At the local level, such efforts can occur in at least three different contexts: a joint project, a joint program, or an interorganizational effort. Joint projects included a community college offering a class focusing on the job openings of a specific employer in a high-growth industry, with the cooperation of that employer. The study team found numerous examples of these joint projects in the published literature. Joint programs included a statewide training program for dislocated workers. In general, these programmatic efforts were more sustained than single projects. In the few years preceding the study, many states had taken such initiatives. In contrast, the interorganizational context did not focus on a single project or program. Rather, the qualifying criterion was that two or more organizations had joined in some arrangement—by forming a joint venture, initiating a consortium, or using interagency agreements among existing organizations—to coordinate training and economic development activities.

With regard to these three contexts, theory and policy relevance played the critical role in the study team's final choice. First, the existing literature indicated that the three contexts were different—cases of one were not to be confused with cases of the others. For instance, programs call for more significant outlays than projects, and interorganizational arrangements may be the most troublesome but can then result in multiple programs and projects.

Second, the literature had given less attention to interorganizational arrangements, even though these had more promise of local capacity-building in the long run. Thus, a local area with a workable interorganizational arrangement may sustain many efforts and may not be as vulnerable to the sporadic nature of single projects or programs.

Third, the study team was interested in advancing knowledge about interorganizational arrangements. In the 1980s, considerable public effort had been made to create public-private partnerships, not just in employment and economic development, but also in many services for disadvantaged population groups—housing, education, social services, health care, mental health care, and community development. (Such interests have continued in the ensuing decades.) Yet, the available literature was shallow with regard to the workings of interorganizational arrangements—how they are formed, what makes them thrive, and how to sustain them.

Finally, a study of interorganizational arrangements also could cover component programs or projects—within the arrangements—as embedded units of analysis. In this way, the study could still touch on all three contexts. For all these reasons, the study team selected the interorganizational arrangement as the unit of analysis to be studied.

Criteria for Selecting Cases

The selection of multiple cases was part of the initial design. However, one constraint was that only a small number of cases could be the subject of study, because the study team wanted to collect data extensively from each interorganizational arrangement—collecting data directly from each of the participating organizations rather than covering just the lead organization. This constraint was again based on theoretical issues because of the study team's desire to investigate the dynamics of each arrangement and not just to apply some input-output framework. The team also suspected that no single organization would have accurate information on what might turn out to be a diversity of programs and projects in each arrangement.

A further constraint was the study's need to inform national policy. Although no representational sampling scheme could be used with such a small number of cases, some distributive factors still demanded attention. Overall, multiple cases were required, but only a small number could be studied, leading to the use of a replication logic to select the final cases.

In using the replication logic, the first selection criterion was that every case had to demonstrate—prior to final case selection—the occurrence of exemplary outcomes. This exemplary case design has been cited as an important use of case studies (Ginsburg, 1989) (see Box 4). The basic replication question would then be whether similar events in each arrangement could account for these outcomes. A second criterion reflected the study's policy concern—some arrangements were to have a federally-supported organization at their center, but other arrangements were to have such organizations in a more peripheral relationship. A third criterion was that the cases were to cover different regions of the country, emphasizing different economic conditions—reflected in the stereotypic notions of "sunbelt," "snowbelt," and "rustbelt."

BOX 4

Exemplary Case Designs

The specific cases to be studied may be selected by following several different rationales, one of which is to select "exemplary" cases. Use of this rationale means that all of the cases will reflect strong, positive examples of the phenomenon of interest (see also Chapter 8 and Box 6). The rationale fits a replication logic well, because your overall investigation may then try to determine whether similar causal events within each case produced these positive outcomes.

The use of the exemplary case design, however, also requires you to determine beforehand whether specific cases indeed have produced exemplary outcomes. Extensive case screening may be needed (see Box 3), and again you must resist permitting the case screening process to become a study in itself.

(For more information, see Yin, 2003, Chapter 2, section on "What Are the Potential Multiple-Case Designs?")

As a result of these considerations, the study team sought six cases. All had to have documented and exemplary outcomes that could survive the study team's screening procedures. Three of the cases would have a key federally-supported organization at their center; the other three would have such an organization in a more peripheral relationship. Together, the six cases would have to cover some distribution of different geographic and economic conditions.

Case Screening

The selection criteria led to a major effort for screening candidate cases. Such an effort is not an unusual adjunct of using the replication logic, and you must plan for sufficient time and resources to support the screening process. A pitfall to be avoided is allowing the screening to be so extensive that the procedure involved doing mini case studies. However, you must be prepared to collect and analyze actual empirical data at this stage.

The study team began this screening process by contacting numerous individuals in the field and consulting available reports and literature. These sources were used to suggest candidates that fit the selection criteria, resulting in a list of 62 nominees. The study team then attempted to contact these nominees both in writing and by phone. The team obtained information on 47 of them.

The information was based on responses to a structured interview of about 45 minutes, using a formal instrument. Each of the candidate arrangements also was encouraged to submit written materials and reports about its operations. The final analysis determined that 22 of the 47 candidates were eligible for further consideration. Table 1.2 lists these 22 candidates (the table also shows the 25 candidates that were considered outside the scope of further interest, and why). From these 22, the study team then selected the final 6, based on the thoroughness of the documentation and accessibility of the site.

Key Lessons

This stage of case study research can assume major proportions in a broader study. In the present illustration, the selection process consumed about 20% of the study's overall resources. Such major investments are not readily appreciated by funding sponsors. However, if the selection process is not properly conducted, even more trouble will result in the ensuing phases of the research.

One option not pursued in this case but implemented in other studies (e.g., COSMOS, 1986) can make the case selection step even more formal and can produce even more useful information. This option is to define the screening process as a formal survey. Its design would depend on the ability to specify a universe and a sampling plan. However, the survey would provide a broader array of quantitative evidence. The final study would therefore contain limited information on a large number of cases as well as intensive information on a smaller number.

CAUSAL CASE STUDIES I: FACTOR THEORIES

One of the most common types of causal theories in social science is the *factor* theory (Downs & Mohr, 1976; Mohr, 1978). Whether explaining some economic outcome (marketplace factors), individual behavior (psychological factors), or social phenomenon (social factors), this paradigm assembles a list of independent variables and determines those that are most highly correlated with the dependent variable. Those independent variables are then considered causally related to the dependent variable. To conduct the analysis and account for such complexities as the interactions among the independent variables, investigators may use factor analysis, regression analysis, and analysis of variance as illustrative statistical techniques.

Table 1.2
Organizations Screened by the Project Team

Category	Name of Organization Contacted	Location/Belt	Type of Area
I. Within Scope of Further Interest:			
Participation by Local Economic Development Agencies	Chester County Office of Employment and Training*	West Chester, PA/Rustbelt	Rural-Suburban
	City of Grand Rapids Development Office*	Grand Rapids, MI/Rustbelt	Urban-Suburban
	Columbus, Indiana Economic Development Board	Columbus, IN/Rustbelt	Rural
	Corpus Christi Area Economic Development Corporation	Corpus Christi, TX/Sunbelt	Urban
	Department of Community and Senior Citizens Services	Los Angeles, CA/Sunbelt	Suburban
	Department of Economic Development	Tacoma, WA/Mixed	Urban
	Office of Economic and Strategic Development	Merced, CA/Sunbelt	Rural
Participation by Private Industry Councils or JTPA Organizations	Northeast Florida Private Industry Council, Inc.*	Jacksonville, FL/Sunbelt	Rural-Mixed
	Pima County Community Services Department*	Tucson, AZ/Sunbelt	Urban-Rural-Suburban
	Portland Private Industry Council	Portland, OR/Mixed	Urban
	Private Industry Council of Snohomish County	Everett, WA/Mixed	Rural-Suburban
	South Coast Private Industry Council	North Quincy, MA/Snowbelt	Suburban
	Susquehanna Region Private Industry Council, Inc.*	Havre de Grace, MD/Mixed	Rural-Suburban
	Western Missouri Private Industry Council	Sedalia, MO/Mixed	Rural
	Yuma Private Industry Council	Yuma, AZ/Sunbelt	Urban-Towns
Participation by Other Self-Standing Organizations	Cascade Business Center Corporation	Portland, OR/Mixed	Urban
	Daytona Beach Community College	Daytona Beach, FL/Sunbelt	Urban-Rural
	Greater Waterbury Chamber of Commerce	Waterbury, CT/Snowbelt	Towns
	Job Opportunities in Nevada	Reno, NV/Sunbelt	Urban-Rural
	Monadnock Training Council	Milford, NH/Snowbelt	Mixed
	Nevada Business Services	Las Vegas, NV/Sunbelt	Urban
	Seattle-King County Economic Development Council*	Seattle, WA/Mixed	Urban-Suburban

(Continued)

Table 1.2
(Continued)

Category	Name of Organization Contacted	Location/Belt	Type of Area
II. Outside Scope of Further Interest:			
Sites With Insufficient Information About Economic Development Activities	Cambridge Instruments, Inc.	Buffalo, NY/Snowbelt	Urban
	Community College of Rhode Island	Lincoln, RI/Snowbelt	Suburban
	Frost Incorporated	Grand Rapids, MI/Rustbelt	Urban
	Hawaii Entrepreneurship Training and Development Institute	Honolulu, HI/Sunbelt	Urban
	Indiana Vocational Technical College	Indianapolis, IN/Rustbelt	Mixed
	Metropolitan Re-Employment Project	St. Louis, MO/Rustbelt	Urban
	National Technological University	Ft. Collins, CO/Snowbelt	Mixed
Single Organizations	Coastal Enterprises, Inc.	Wiscasset, ME/Snowbelt	Rural
Operating Both Training and Economic Development Activities	Cooperative Home Care Associates	Bronx, NY/Snowbelt	Urban
	Esperanza Unida, Inc.	Milwaukee, WI/Snowbelt	Urban
	Focus Hope	Detroit, MI/Rustbelt	Urban
	Women's Economic Development Corporation	St. Paul, MN/Snowbelt	Urban-Suburban
	The Business Development and Training Center at Great Valley	Malvern, PA/Rustbelt	Rural
Training Institutions Operating Both Training and Economic Development Activities	Catonsville Community College	Baltimore, MD/Rustbelt	Urban-Suburban
	Highlander Economic Development Center	New Market, TN/Mixed	Rural
	Job Services of Florida	Perry, FL/Sunbelt	Rural
	Luzerne County Community College	Nanticoke, PA/Rustbelt	Urban-Suburban
	Massachusetts Career Development Institute	Springfield, MA/Snowbelt	Suburban
	Niagara County Community College	Sanborn, NY/Snowbelt	Mostly Rural
	Pensacola Junior College	Pensacola, FL/Sunbelt	Metropolitan-Rural
State-Level Operations	Arizona Dept. of Economic Security	Phoenix, AZ/Sunbelt	Mostly Rural
	Bluegrass State Skills Corporation	Frankfort, KY/Mixed	Mixed
	Delaware Development Office	Dover, DE/Rustbelt	Urban-Rural
	State of Iowa Dept. of Economic Development	Des Moines, IA/Snowbelt	Urban-Rural
	North Carolina Department of Community Colleges	Raleigh, NC/Sunbelt	Mixed

The use of factor theories has its counterpart in case study research, although such an application is not desired. However, if factor theories—and not causally linked explanatory theories—are the state of knowledge on a given topic, a case study investigator may not be able to avoid this application. Many causal case studies have had to be done under these conditions. The following example was therefore included to show how a factor theory could be incorporated into a case study and also to illustrate the limitations of this application.

The Research Issue: How to Attract High-Tech Firms to New Locations

Local economic development theory is a good example of a topic still dominated by factor theories. Firms are said to be influenceable in their decisions to locate or relocate due to the following illustrative types of general factors:

- The availability of venture capital and other forms of start-up financing
- The local tax structure, including costs due to taxes and incentives due to tax breaks
- The physical characteristics of a place (physical capital)
- The labor force characteristics of a place (human capital)
- The governing laws and regulations covering wages, the formation of unions, depreciation, and numerous other items
- The preferences of key executives and their spouses

In each general factor can be created long lists of specific factors, and local governments try to use these specific factors as policy tools in attracting firms. The most attractive locale is the one that can maximize as many factors as possible. However, rarely are these factors expressed in some coherent, causal model that would represent a truly explanatory model of why firms relocate.

The illustrative study investigated a contemporary offshoot of this traditional situation by focusing on high-tech firms (COSMOS, 1985). The study asked whether high-tech firms respond to the same factors as any industrial firm or whether some other factors also are important. The study's goal was to identify such distinctive factors, if any, to provide advice to local governments desirous of attracting high-tech firms and not just industrial firms—a goal glorified by such developmental successes as California's Silicon Valley, North Carolina's Research Triangle, and Boston's Route 128 corridor.

The study could have been designed as a survey or secondary analysis of economic data, both of which have been common ways of investigating this topic. However, such investigations do not permit in-depth examination of the factors themselves, focusing mainly on the outcome of whether a firm has decided to relocate. In contrast, the illustrative case study was intended to examine the factors more closely, thereby requiring data collection from a variety of sources and not from just the firm itself.

Data Collection and Findings From Firms
in Nine High-Tech or Industrial Parks

To satisfy this objective, the study team conducted case studies of nine high-tech or industrial parks. The team began with a long list of potential initiatives (or factors) used to attract firms. From this long list, the team determined the initiatives actually used by each park to attract firms, through interviews with the park's developers and local economic development officials as well as through an analysis of documentary evidence. The team then surveyed the firms in each park to ascertain the rationales for their locational choices and to confirm whether these mirrored the parks' initiatives. In all, the team conducted nine case studies and surveyed 232 firms, with responses from 200 of them (86%).[1]

The responses from the firms were initially used to confirm whether the parks were high-tech parks (parks dominated by high-tech firms) or industrial parks (parks dominated by industrial but not high-tech firms). Table 1.3 shows that Parks A, B, F, and I had more firms in research businesses than in manufacturing businesses and were therefore considered high-tech parks. Conversely, Parks C, D, E, G, and H had more firms in manufacturing rather than research businesses and were therefore considered industrial parks.

The case studies were used to determine the initiatives (factors) undertaken by each of the nine parks to attract firms. Overall, certain basic factors (such as location near markets or transportation access) prevailed in all nine parks. However, in comparison to the five industrial parks, the four high-tech parks were found to have undertaken the following additional initiatives:

1. Exclusionary zoning or restrictive covenants, to produce a campuslike environment

2. University initiatives, to create collaborative efforts or personnel exchange between firms and local universities

3. Special utility capabilities, whether related to electrical power or telephone lines

Table 1.3

Number of Firms in Each Park, by Type of Business Conducted

Park	Research	Light Manufacturing	Heavy Manufacturing and Distribution	Other	Total
A	8	0	0	16	24
B	7	2	0	9	18
C	0	1	8	6	15
D	0	12	6	8	26
E	2	6	3	5	16
F	8	1	0	10	19
G	3	3	3	14	23
H	0	1	2	1	4
I	21	2	0	3	26
Totals	49	28	22	72	171

The identification of these additional initiatives permitted the study team to conclude that high-tech parks had pursued policies distinct from those of industrial parks.

The survey responses from the firms were analyzed to determine whether preference for these same initiatives distinguished high-tech businesses from industrial firms. The results supported the importance of the university and utility initiatives to the acceptable degree of statistical significance, but they were neutral regarding the importance of a campuslike environment. Despite the lack of confirmation for this last initiative, the study team concluded that real estate developments wanting to attract high-tech firms should focus on the three initiatives in addition to those used to attract industrial firms.

Key Lessons

This example demonstrates the use of a factor theory in a causal case study. The case study was able to identify individual initiatives to attract high-tech firms. Nevertheless, the limitations of this approach, with only a factor theory available for testing, also should be evident:

- No causal understanding could be developed regarding a firm's actual decision-making process in deciding to relocate.
- The initiatives (or factors) could not be ranked in any order of importance.
- The potential interactions between factors—and any determination of whether these were part of the same, more general, factor—could not be determined.

Possibly the latter two of these shortcomings can be overcome by using some method other than the case study. Factor theories generally thrive when there are sufficient data points to conduct extensive analysis among the factors, thereby favoring survey or secondary analysis rather than case study designs. The ensuing factor analysis or regression analysis could then be directed at determining the relative strength or importance of each factor, as well as at the interactions between factors. At the same time, even when there are sufficient data points, factor theories are inherently weak in developing an understanding of the underlying causal processes.

CAUSAL CASE STUDIES II: EXPLANATORY THEORIES

In comparison to factor theories, explanatory theories are more suitable for designing and doing causal case studies. In fact, the more complex and multivariate the explanatory theory, the better. The case study analysis can then take advantage of pattern-matching techniques. Unfortunately, viable explanatory theories do not always exist for the topics covered by case studies, so investigators cannot always use this approach. However, a study conducted on the topic of research utilization benefited from the prior existence of several complex and rival theories—readily translatable into operational terms—and illustrates well the advantages of the approach.

The Research Issue: How and Why
Do Research Findings Get Into Practical Use?

The illustrative study focused on the key policy objective of making research more useful (Yin & Moore, 1988). Nine case studies were selected in which a funded research project was the unit of analysis. All projects were on a topic of natural hazards research and were known to have been conducted in an exemplary manner, leading to significant scientific publications, but the projects varied in their utilization outcomes. The illustrative case study assessed and confirmed these outcomes, but it then went further to examine the explanations for these outcomes. Such explanations in turn were based on three major rival theories in the literature on research utilization: a knowledge-driven theory, a problem-solving theory, and a social-interaction theory.

The *knowledge-driven theory* stipulates that ideas and discoveries from basic research eventually result in inventions or advances in applied research, often leading to commercial products or services. Utilization is therefore the result of a linear sequence of activities following a "technology-push" process in which researchers continually produce the new ideas that get put into use.

The *problem-solving theory* also follows a linear sequence. However, the stipulated activities begin with the identification of a problem by some individual or organization in need of a solution, not by a research investigator. Even if the problem has been poorly or incorrectly articulated, it is communicated to a research investigator, whose task is to conduct the research needed to identify, test, and assess alternative solutions to the problem. The investigator also may redefine the problem. However, utilization is explained by a "demand-pull" process, reflecting the fact that the ultimate user of the research (a) helped to define the initial problem and (b) is therefore waiting for and prepared to implement the solution (assuming a viable one emerges from the research).

The *social-interaction theory* does not stipulate a linear process. Rather, this theory claims that in high-utilization environments, research producers and users belong to overlapping professional networks with ongoing communications. The communications need not focus on any particular research endeavor; instead, the objective of communication is to assure that researchers and users are exposed to each other's worlds and needs, producing a rich "marketplace of ideas" (Yin & Gwaltney, 1981). Such communications can have serendipitous effects. For instance, research investigators may alter the focus of their studies or the early design of their research, based on dialogues with users. Or, as another example, users can project their future needs to reflect a sensitivity to ongoing research developments. In this milieu, utilization ultimately occurs because the continuous flow of communications increasingly leads to good matches between existing needs and emerging new research.

These three theories produced two critical conditions for the illustrative case study. First, they led to a predicted and complex course of events when utilization occurred, and the absence of those events when utilization did not occur. The existence of this course of events could then be traced in individual cases, with a pattern-matching analysis comparing the hypothesized with the actual course of events (Trochim, 1989; Yin, 2003). The complex nature of the course makes the relevant evidence more discernible. Second, the three theories led to rival courses—events that are nearly mutually exclusive. Empirical support for one theory therefore could not be used to argue for support of another theory. In this sense, although the case studies were retrospectively conducted, the data actually permitted the testing of rival theories.

Results

The nine case studies followed a replication design—six cases having strong utilization outcomes, although the research covered different academic fields, and three cases having negligible utilization outcomes. The main result was that those cases with the most extensive and diverse array of utilization outcomes were all found to have key ingredients of the social-interaction theory: Existing professional networks created rich, ongoing producer-user dialogue. In some of the cases, professional associations facilitated the exchange of ideas. In other cases, the exchange was simply the result of an active and communicative principal investigator. Overall, communications started earlier than and continued far beyond the ending of a specific research project, in comparison to those projects with minimal utilization outcomes.

Key Lessons

The main lesson from this experience is that the presence of explanatory theories can facilitate theory testing with a rich and extensive data collection effort, including qualitative and quantitative evidence. Each of the nine cases was investigated by reviewing pertinent documents, interviewing a wide array of individuals including actual or potential users of the research, and observing the actual research processes or products. The case study protocol, tightly geared to testing the three theories, assured that the diverse data collection would involve converging lines of inquiry and triangulation of the evidence.

A key aspect of the theories was their complexity. This permitted pattern matching of a series or sequence of events as the main analytic tactic in each of the cases. Without the theories or their complexity, data collection might have been undisciplined and pattern matching impossible. In this respect, the case study method may rely differently on explanatory theories than do other methods. Whereas other methods may prefer single-variable theories and the incremental development of causal links over a series of studies, pattern matching in case study analysis permits case studies to test multiple-variable, complex causal explanations in a single study.

DESCRIPTIVE CASE STUDIES

Rules about the development of descriptive theory have generally been overlooked in favor of rules about explanatory theory (see Box 5). Yet

---

BOX 5

Theories for Descriptive Case Studies

References to the use of theory usually involve the formation of hypotheses of cause-effect relationships. These theories would therefore be considered relevant to explanatory case studies.

Theories, however, also can be important for descriptive case studies. A descriptive theory is not an expression of a cause-effect relationship. Rather, a descriptive theory covers the scope and depth of the object (case) being described. If you were to describe an individual, an organization, or some other possible subject of a case study, where should your description start, and where should it end? What should your description include, and what might it exclude? The criteria used to answer these questions would represent your "theory" of what needs to be described. This theory should be openly stated ahead of time, should be subject to review and debate, and will later serve as the design for a descriptive case study. A thoughtful theory will help to produce a sound descriptive case study.

(For more information, see Yin, 2003, Chapter 2, section on "The Role of Theory in Design Work.")

---

many investigations have description as their main objective. Such circumstances still call for some theory to determine the priorities for data collection. The typical atheoretic statement, "Let's collect information about everything" does not work, and the investigator without a descriptive theory will soon encounter enormous problems in limiting the scope of the study.

Multiple-Case Design

An illustrative use of descriptive theory was a study on special education (education for students with disabilities) in four states—Massachusetts, South Dakota, North Dakota, and New Jersey (Pyecha et al., 1988). The case study analysis followed a pattern-matching procedure: Data about each state's activities were compared with two rival, idealized, and theoretic patterns. The prediction was that two states (Massachusetts and South Dakota) would follow one pattern but not the other, whereas the other two states (North Dakota and New Jersey) would have the reverse result.

Thus the case study design, even for a descriptive study, followed a replication logic. Without sufficiently strong theory, the differences or similarities between states would be difficult to interpret. In other words, the role of theory was to specify the differences between the two types of states that would be considered substantively critical. The key to the study design was the detailed and prior development of the rival theoretic patterns, portrayed as alternative scenarios. Experts helped to develop and review these scenarios (or descriptive theories) against which the actual data were compared.

The Research Issue: Categorical Versus Noncategorical Education

Elementary and secondary special education commonly occurs in *categorical*, self-contained classes. In this arrangement, students are first categorized according to disability; those with similar disabilities are grouped and taught together for some if not all of their classes. This philosophy of education argues that (a) different disabilities arise from different etiologies, and (b) students with different disabilities have different learning needs; therefore, (c) different instructional methods must be developed and tailored to each type of disability. Furthermore, grouping the students according to their disabilities leads to more homogeneous classrooms, making instructional practices easier.

Logical as the argument appears, an alternative educational philosophy is that the educational needs and learning processes of disabled students are basically no different from each other or from those of students without disabilities. Major differences may arise in the levels of achievement, but separate instructional methods are not relevant. Thus, except for limited supplemental situations, students with and without disabilities should share the same classrooms, curriculum, and instruction.

This alternative philosophy is known as *noncategorical* education, whose implementation produces several benefits in comparison to categorical systems. First and foremost, a noncategorical system permits students with disabilities to remain in neighborhood schools, whereas categorical systems can lead to special classes (indeed, special schools) in remote locations, due to scalar requirements. Second, a noncategorical system is fully integrated with the regular education system, whereas a categorical system produces a dual system (one for regular education students and the other for students with disabilities). Third, a noncategorical system can avoid the potential negative consequences of labeling a student as having disabilities.

Debate over these contrasting philosophies in education circles has been strong. Current federal policy tends to favor the development of categorical systems, but states are charged with delivering public education services and must therefore design their own policies. During the 1970s and 1980s, two states chose to implement noncategorical systems—Massachusetts and South Dakota. A study of how such systems differ, in practice, from categorical systems had to be conceived as a multiple-case study.

The purpose of the study was not to determine which system was better. Instead, the purpose was descriptive—to define current practices in using noncategorical systems, determining whether such practices are indeed different from those in categorical systems.

Units of Analysis and Selection of Cases

Because state policy is the organizing force for all local public education, the state was the main unit of analysis. The study had to include Massachusetts and South Dakota automatically, because they were the only states with noncategorical systems. For comparison purposes, the study team selected two geographically similar states to be paired with these first two states—New Jersey with Massachusetts and North Dakota with South Dakota.

In each state, educational services are delivered by local systems. Therefore, a sample of 28 such local systems was also selected for study in the four chosen states, representing an embedded unit of analysis. Data from the local systems were needed to ensure that differences in state policies actually resulted in different practices at the local level. For this reason, the selection of these 28 local systems was based on a state official's informed judgment that a district was implementing the state's policies with fidelity, so the selection of local systems again reflected a replication logic.

Development of Descriptive Scenarios

The design of the study required the careful development of idealized scenarios of the two types of systems. Draft scenarios were initially based on the research literature and consultation with experts. An expert advisory panel then reviewed the drafts, making important comments and modifications. The completed scenarios became the basis for developing data collection protocols.

The importance of these scenarios in the study design cannot be underestimated. Descriptive studies typically fail to specify a priori the critical ingredients of the phenomenon to be described. Data collection then rambles as a result, and the ensuing case study may even contain undesirable, circular reasoning—the final description constituting a contaminated combination of what may have been expected and what was found. In contrast, the scenarios were intended to recapture the essence of what constituted categorical or noncategorical systems. The driving question underlying the development of the scenarios was, "What specific educational practices must a local school system have, to be considered an example of categorical (or noncategorical) education?" The scenarios and their practices defined the relevant data collection: The presence or absence of a series of practices (10 for categorical and 17 for noncategorical education) was to be tracked in each of the 28 local school systems.

Note that under this scheme, unanticipated findings are not precluded. Revelatory or important information found outside the original scenarios can still be collected and analyzed later. However, the initial scenarios provide major support in structuring the data collection in the first place and avoiding an unending collection process.

Results

For most but not all of the proposed features, the 28 school systems in the four states followed the predicted pattern: Local systems in the two states with categorical policies were more like each other than like those in the two states with noncategorical policies. At the same time, a subset of features was not found, as postulated by the scenarios, to distinguish local systems in the categorical states from those in the noncategorical states. Examples were a practice where the data revealed that special education was not located in special facilities, even in categorical states—mainly due to federal policies. The data also revealed that principals did not control special education in their schools, even in the noncategorical states. The overall findings were therefore used to modify the original scenarios on the basis of the empirical findings to describe how noncategorical systems differed from categorical systems.

Key Lessons

One lesson was that the scenarios could not have been developed had there not been an extensive literature and policy debate on categorical versus noncategorical systems. The literature and debate provided an array of practices, in highly operational terms, to be tested in the field. Many other topics of interest to researchers may not have such rich sources, and the descriptive theory cannot be developed as easily before a case study is to be done. Under such circumstances, the final result may border on an exploratory rather than descriptive case study.

A second lesson concerned the benefit of having rival theories. Without the categorical system as a contrast, any description of the noncategorical system could have become undisciplined and spilled over to other aspects of school system operations not critical to their noncategorical nature. The availability of a rival theory helped to avoid such an expansive tendency, instead focusing data collection on the practices important to noncategorical systems.

CONCLUSIONS

These five illustrations show the multiple applications of theory to case study research and evaluations. Critical to all illustrations was the development of such theory prior to the conduct of the study. Furthermore, such development frequently required substantial time, resources, and expertise.

This approach to case studies mimics that used in most experimental science, where expert knowledge of prior research and careful hypothesis development precede actual experimentation. The approach therefore requires that case study investigators be well informed about the topics of inquiry and not simply dependent on a methodological tool kit. Moreover, the approach gives investigators an opportunity to reveal (and minimize) substantive biases that may affect the design and conduct of a case study. Finally, the approach produces case studies that can be part of a cumulative body of knowledge and not just isolated empirical inquiries.

NOTE

1. The complete case study design therefore was described as a multiple-case study of nine parks, with a survey of firms being an embedded unit of analysis. The entire study design represents a strong example of combining the use of qualitative and quantitative methods in the same case study.

PART II

Descriptive Case Studies

2

A Case Study of a Neighborhood Organization

Neighborhood organizations exist throughout the country and have been important vehicles for neighborhood development and resident participation. Strong interest in these organizations has continued among social scientists and policy analysts alike. Case studies of the organizations frequently appear in the literature.

This chapter presents one such case study. By now, the particular neighborhood organization has historical significance because nationally it was among the leading such organizations some 40 years ago. The case study also takes place against the backdrop of federal initiatives that were new and innovative at the time: the antipoverty and Model Cities programs. The case study therefore not only captures the work of a major neighborhood organization but also has the flavor of the earlier federal era.

Methodologically, the case study was deliberately designed to present answers to a series of questions. The questions reflect the interest of those who represented a special entity, the U.S. National Commission on Neighborhoods, that existed in the late 1970s. Inclusion of the questions in a case study protocol used to collect data from over 40 such neighborhood organizations assured the commissioners that an entire series of case studies would address their concerns. Although the resulting case studies were rather mechanically composed as a result, the format also made it easier for

AUTHOR'S NOTE: This chapter is a highly condensed version of a case study that appeared in *People, Building Neighborhoods*, National Commission on Neighborhoods, U.S. Government Printing Office, Washington, D.C., March 1979. The case is 1 of more than 40 such case studies based on a similar research design and research procedure developed by Robert K. Yin. To keep the chapter a manageable length, substantial portions of the original case study have been omitted, mainly shown in those instances where a posed textual question has no response. Despite the omitted responses, all the questions are included here to help readers understand the full flow of the original case study's logic. The original and complete case study was written by Kenneth Snipes. The portion presented in this chapter has been lightly edited for readability.

BOX 6

Developing a Case Study Database

The question-and-answer format in this case study on a neighborhood organization is not just a way of presenting a case study report. The format also may be used to organize a database from which a more interesting and compelling case study can be composed.

Preserving the database in its question-and-answer form, reflecting the questions from the case study protocol, is comparable to the assembling of a survey database and strengthens any subsequent case study. The most formal version of a case study database would contain numerous citations, indicating the specific source of the data, such as a particular document, interview, archive, or date and place of a field observation. Thus the current case study of a neighborhood organization could have been used as either the final case study (as presented here) or the database for a separately composed case study.

(For more information, see Yin, 2003, Chapter 4, section on "Three Principles of Data Collection: Principle 2.")

---

the commissioners (and other readers) to find the answers to the questions of concern. Furthermore, as the present chapter shows, the mechanical organization of the case study did not preclude inclusion of a rather rich and in-depth description of each organization (see Box 6). The format also facilitated the writing of the cases, as the case study investigators could assemble their notes and data to answer each question rather than struggling with a more fluid, though potentially more creative, reporting structure.

Overall, the chapter illustrates a descriptive case study organized according to a series of questions and answers. Most of the evidence is about events, representing qualitative rather than quantitative evidence. However, later chapters will show how case studies can incorporate quantitative as well as qualitative evidence (see Box 7).

INITIATION AND STRUCTURE OF THE ORGANIZATION

Organizational Origins

1. In what year did the organization come into being? Jeff-Vander-Lou, Inc. (JVL), formally came into being on October 24, 1966. On March 29,

---

BOX 7

Qualitative and Quantitative Research

The dichotomy between qualitative and quantitative research has become a caricature in the social sciences. Qualitative research, including case studies, is characterized as being "soft" social science, dealing with inadequate evidence. Quantitative research is considered to be hard-nosed, data-driven, outcome-oriented, and truly scientific.

This book assumes on the contrary that case study research can be *either* qualitative *or* quantitative. The characteristics are therefore not attributes of two competing types of research. Instead, they are attributes of types of data. *Qualitative data* cannot readily be converted to numerical values. Such data can be represented by categorical data, by perceptual and attitudinal dimensions (e.g., color perception), and by real-life events. The case study in this chapter is dominated by qualitative data.

Such a focus on the type of data also avoids the unproductive debate between qualitative and quantitative research. Qualitative research also can be hard-nosed, data-driven, outcome-oriented, and truly scientific. Similarly, quantitative research can be soft because of inappropriate numbers; it may also be based on inadequate evidence. These are attributes of good and poor research and not of a dichotomy between two different types of research.

(For more information, see Yin, 2003, Chapter 1, section on "Variations in Case Studies.")

1967, its articles of incorporation were officially amended, granting JVL broader legal capacity to engage in building, rebuilding, purchasing, selling, leasing, investing of funds, and other such activities geared to more specific undertakings in terms of its goal of community renewal.

Jeff-Vander-Lou, Inc., evolved out of the 19th Ward Beautification Committee created in mid-1964 in response to Lady Bird Johnson's efforts to encourage the beautification of America. The group was initially headed by local officials (19th Ward alderman and committeeman). However, later in 1964, three community activists were elected as its first major officers. The name *Jeff-Vander-Lou* is derived from three principal streets that bound the area—*Jeff* from Jefferson Avenue, *Vander* from Vandeventer Avenue, and *Lou* from St. Louis Avenue.

2. What caused its creation and who or what was the main source of support in the creation? Jeff-Vander-Lou, Inc., was created as a result of a series of issues, events, and the union of the three principal individuals who emerged from community meetings, marches, and other such neighborhood activities. These three leaders were Macler C. Shepard, Reverend Hubert Schwartzentruber, and Florence Aritha Spotts.

Macler Shepard, owner of an upholstery shop, had been twice displaced by urban renewal projects. He decided to move no more. He ran unsuccessfully for 19th Ward committeeman. A committeeman is a nonpaid party functionary who is responsible for getting the vote out. In the spring of 1964, following the shooting of a youth by a police officer in a neighborhood schoolyard, Shepard had mobilized a citizens' protest. It grew into a march of 5,000 to 8,000 people, which started from the Jeff-Vander-Lou area and went through the Pruitt-Igoe housing project (since demolished) to police headquarters. Subsequently, Shepard served as spokesman in joint meetings with officials.

Hubert Schwartzentruber, a young Mennonite minister from a small rural section of Canada, was sent by his church to the near North Side black community of St. Louis. Until that time, he never had been in a large city or had any personal contact with black people. He succeeded the pastor of a black Mennonite Church located near Shepard's upholstery shop. Schwartzentruber set up a coffeehouse called *The Handle*, where people from the neighborhood could discuss problems and concerns. It became a meeting place for residents and others interested in issues affecting poor and black people.

Florence Aritha Spotts, a retired schoolteacher, was among those who frequented *The Handle*. She had a reputation as an organizer and critic of politicians and the political process. She said she would fight anything she thought was wrong.

These three people joined forces in 1964 and were elected to major offices of the 19th Ward Beautification Committee. They attempted to use that committee to develop community improvement projects and, in particular, a housing rehabilitation program.

In an attempt by Mayor Cervantes's administration to befriend the 19th Ward neighborhood, paint was delivered to it. However, the 19th Ward Beautification Committee sent back the paint (along with a strongly worded message to the mayor), because it only could be used for the exteriors of buildings. The large number of deteriorating houses indicated that more serious help was necessary. Another promise of assistance for the neighborhood came from the Cervantes administration in the form of Operation: Big-Sweep, a clean-up campaign scheduled to begin in the 19th Ward in late 1965. When the mayor pushed an oversized symbolic broom, the handle broke. The JVL neighborhood still ranks clean-up, street paving, and sidewalk repair (along with other city services) among its top priorities in support of its housing development efforts.

During this same period (1964-1966), another government program designed to rescue poor people and neighborhood was being implemented. The U.S. Office of Economic Opportunity (OEO) was preparing for antipoverty programs in the Yeatman District. The geographical boundaries of this area were much the same as the area identified with the 19th Ward Beautification Committee. The OEO program was established through its local agency, the Human Development Corporation (HDC), which in turn delegated implementation responsibilities to the Urban League of Greater St. Louis. The Urban League's first task was to organize a neighborhood advisory council to direct the efforts and resources available through OEO. During the process of organizing, conflicts surfaced between the existing, more traditional Urban League Federation of Block Units (block clubs) and the leadership of the 19th Ward Beautification Committee.

Against this backdrop of confrontation with the administration of Mayor Cervantes and the local entanglements of the antipoverty and, soon to come, federal Model Cities programs, two specific issues contributed most to the creation of Jeff-Vander-Lou, Inc. Both issues surfaced in 1966.

First, the city announced a major $79.3 million bond issue and asked for citywide support. The bond issue provided improvements in most areas of the city *except* the JVL neighborhood, according to JVL respondents and writings. These facts became apparent after investigation by the Urban League organizers who were working closely with the beautification committee. Protests were made to the city, but the officials would not alter or commit the bond issue to specifically include the 19th Ward Beautification Committee/Yeatman area. JVL respondents who were active at that time indicated that the city's refusal strengthened the belief that the neighborhood was actually scheduled for complete demolition and redevelopment. At the base of this fear was that the area would become the site of new industrial development and permit the construction of a north-south distributor highway.

The determined efforts of Shepard and the JVL community, together with a group from the predominantly white South Side, forced the defeat of the bond issue in November 1966. For example, the city promoted the passage with a booklet titled *Let's Do It.* The JVL community countered with a mimeographed booklet called *Let's Don't,* which pointed out that some proposals provided for and passed in a 1955 bond issue were duplicated in the 1966 bond proposal. Also, the JVL community strongly opposed the north-south highway that could be constructed with passage of the bond issue. According to Shepard, the highway would further divide the black community, displace many people relocated two or three times before because of urban renewal, and be of primary benefit to county residents rather than those who lived in the city.

The second issue came after the bond issue failed. In late 1966, JVL, together with the Urban League outreach staff, met with the St. Louis Building Commissioner to protest the lack of housing code enforcement in the JVL area. Again there was refusal by the city to apply its resources to problems and concerns identified by those in the community. The city officials stated that buildings in the "slum areas" were inspected only on a specific complaint rather than on a community-wide basis.

Homeowners in the JVL area began to submit complaints against violators, but the complainants then found that their own homes were being inspected. Respondents indicated that absentee owners were receiving minor fines, but owner-occupants were ordered to make extensive repairs. The legal and economic pressures on the residents threatened to discontinue the demand for community-wide code enforcement.

Workers in the JVL community spent the next three weeks collecting about 1,200 complaints against 13 real estate dealers who owned or managed 85% of the property in the neighborhood. In this instance, all the complaints were filed by persons who lived outside the area. Later, the Building Commissioner announced that 75% of the area was "unfit for human habitation." Families were evicted. As the city evicted families, Jeff-Vander-Lou moved them back in and, in addition, announced that it was setting up "refugee camps" in churches, community centers, and other such places.

Meanwhile, riots began in other major cities. The building commissioner stopped the evictions, public officials sought to negotiate a settlement, and JVL exacted a promise of no further urban renewal. This action provided JVL with the opportunity to purchase the structurally sound abandoned houses and to rehabilitate and sell them to the residents.

Simultaneously (in late 1966), Shepard, Schwartzentruber, and Spotts—along with the Reverend Donald Register of the United Presbyterian Church, the Urban League staff organizers, and other neighborhood people—planned for the creation of Jeff-Vander-Lou, Inc. (incorporation of JVL), designed to be an independent citizen-controlled organization. It was incorporated on October 24, 1966. Macler Shepard was elected president of its board of directors.

Despite the creation of JVL as a separate organization, its supporters and directors continued their attempts at influencing the use of OEO resources through the Yeatman Advisory Council.

The struggle for control of the Advisory Council resulted in the disqualification of the election results on three different occasions by the Human Development Corporation (HDC). During this period, JVL gained neighborhood support to act as the OEO Yeatman district advisory council. According to a JVL administrative assistant, HDC was against JVL controlling the Yeatman council, and elections were held until the JVL influence was diluted. The executive director of the Yeatman Corporation recalled that the disqualifications resulted from JVL protests and their resistance to open elections with a broad-based council, as required by OEO. In the spring of 1967, prior to the formation of the Yeatman Corporation but following the incorporation of Jeff-Vander-Lou, the Urban League terminated its staff organizers. Several of those individuals continue to play key roles in JVL today.

Finally, in the fall of 1967, election results were certified. The JVL constituency obtained 13 seats and the remaining 47 were won by others with no prior experience in neighborhood organizations, according to the Yeatman Corporation's executive director. During 1967, the JVL constituency on the Yeatman Council discovered that it could not adequately influence the council's decisions and actions.

3. What was the original source of funding? Jeff-Vander-Lou, Inc., had no formal funding sources at its creation. According to Macler Shepard and other respondents, personal funds from the leadership itself were used to cover various operational expenses. Some printing and other such costs were paid for by neighborhood people, including the Franklin Avenue Businessmen's Association. The Urban League staff organizers provided primary technical assistance from 1965 to 1967. Because funding had been from private (not public) sources during its initial period, JVL was able to engage in politically active matters that it considered vital to the survival of the neighborhood.

According to a JVL staff member, the first house renovated was undertaken in 1967 at a cost of about $18,000. The financing of the two-family dwelling was provided through funds loaned by the Lindell Trust Company, which has offices in the area. Additionally, financial assistance came from local businessmen (the Franklin Avenue Businessmen's Association, now called the Martin Luther King Redevelopment Association, after the street name was changed) and other neighborhood people.

Once under way in 1967, JVL, Inc., received a $30,000 interest-free loan for housing rehabilitation from the Mennonite Church (the Mennonite Mutual Aid Fund). Also, the Mennonites' Minority Ministries Council made a grant of $30,000 to hire a construction supervisor for a 3-year period. The Mennonite Disaster Services sent skilled craftsmen into the JVL neighborhood to rehabilitate houses, and the Illinois Mennonite Youth Fellowship raised funds to help purchase and rehabilitate a house.

According to one respondent, a professor at Washington University, college students from that school and others have worked in the JVL area since 1967. The type of technical assistance provided by students and faculty alike included grant development, research, and analysis. For instance, individuals from the university researched state requirements for day care programs (e.g., the needed ratio of space to number of students, nutrition, criteria for selection of youngsters, and financing of day care services).

Another example of outside resources was the funding of a trip to Washington, D.C., by the Franklin Avenue Businessmen's Association for JVL representatives to present their proposals to officials of the U.S. Departments of Housing and Urban Development (HUD); Health, Education, and Welfare (HEW) [now Health and Human Services]; and Labor. All early proposals were rejected. HUD, in particular, made it clear that JVL needed to acquire experience in handling funds and to demonstrate the capacity to undertake housing rehabilitation projects before it would seriously consider JVL's proposals.

Among outside technical resources available to JVL in 1968 and 1969 was a Mennonite farmer from Washington State who had special expertise in large-scale projects and the ability to figure out government regulations. While working in St. Louis, he supplemented his income by teaching. According to the pastor of the Mennonite Church, the clergy also has been important to JVL in getting ideas into workable form.

In 1967, a successful St. Louis businessman took a special interest in JVL. According to an article in the *Globe Democrat* (December 5, 1977), "The founder and president of the Tier-Rack Corporation and Arrowhead Products Company set up a tax deductible corporation, called the Arrowhead Foundation, to provide Jeff-Vander-Lou with seed money for constructing a medical office, warehouse space, and a site for tenant relocation and homeowner training." A report in the *St. Louis Post-Dispatch* (November 15, 1976) indicated that the Arrowhead Foundation's founder called the private sector "tools" and the community residents, "craftsmen." The article stated that in 6 years, Arrowhead had given Jeff-Vander-Lou about $1 million in grants and interest-free loans.

4. Was either mandated citizen participation or formal, legal grants of authority involved in initiating the target organization?

5. What was the early orientation of the organization?

6. What was the organization's main leadership structure?

7. What was the organization's membership and structure?

Organizational Evolution

8. How has the organization changed since the early days? The changes in JVL have been in terms of size of staff, intensity, and greater organizational structure stemming from the general increase in the number of activities, programs, and projects. The intensity of JVL's housing development activities led to the creation of a separately incorporated entity in 1970 called JVL Housing Corporation. JVL Housing is exempted under IRS Section 501(c)(3), so that the organization has received tax-deductible contributions that have boosted its housing development efforts. JVL Housing evolved from negotiations with HUD, which (during 1967-1970) insisted on a cosponsor for a particular housing development of 74 new units under HUD's 236 rental housing program. Businesses and foundations gave extensive support following the establishment of JVL Housing.

Structural change came with the staffing and funding requirements of each JVL, Inc., program component, also resulting in the functional spread of JVL. Because JVL had set its mission along comprehensive activity lines from the very beginning, these developments are seen as fulfilling the neighborhood plan rather than as changes. The evolutionary direction, therefore, has been one of overcoming setbacks as JVL has attempted to carry out its reinvestment and survival plans for its neighborhood.

Outside the housing field, important transitions by JVL have been as follows:

- In 1969, JVL set up an employment screening and referral office for the Brown Shoe Company, which had built a new factory in the JVL area.
- Early in the 1970s, JVL made public improvements through the Model Cities program, working with the Franklin Avenue Businessmen's Association.
- Also in 1970, JVL established a housing management program.
- In 1973, day care activities were formalized.
- Later in 1973, the JVL Senior Citizens' Center was started.
- In the spring of 1974, JVL published its first paper, called the *Jeff-Vander-Look*. In November 1975, the paper was reorganized with *Proud* magazine's assistance and renamed *JVL News*.
- In 1976, JVL began its Summer Youth Program, funded through the U.S. Department of Labor. An economic development staff was added during that same year.
- In 1977, the JVL Communications Center, an outgrowth of the summer program, received funding.

Each of these activities, along with many issue-oriented tasks, caused changes in the organization, in turn helping to assure both supervision and continuity by providing for professional staffing and appropriate facilities. Throughout, JVL's geographic boundaries have remained the same, and housing development continues to be a high priority.

9. What were the events that led to these changes?

10. Overall, has the organization become more independent or dependent?

REVITALIZATION ACTIVITIES AND THEIR SUPPORT

11. What activities have been completed or are currently under way? JVL has had many accomplishments, especially in housing development:

- *1968:* Renovated first building, a 12-room house; completed five housing units repaid through a HUD mortgage insurance program; brought 10 private insurance companies together, agreeing to spread the risk of loss among themselves through a rotation process, to meet JVL's insurance needs to cover 88 units until the Missouri Fair Plan was created in 1969-1970
- *1969:* Rehabilitated "Opportunity House," a complex consisting of six apartments completed at a cost of $85,000; renovated the Sheridan Medical Building, which was then operated by doctors for the benefit of the JVL area; convinced the Brown Group, Inc., to build a shoe factory in the JVL neighborhood and began handling employment screening and referral for a peak employment level of 450 workers
- *1967-70:* Completed a total of 81 units under a HUD program; units were sold to families in the community with interest subsidy ranging from 1% to 3%
- *1970:* Set up housing management component with a grant from the national Self-development of People Committee of the Presbyterian Church, allowing for the payment of salaries for the manager of the Spotts Apartments, a chief executive, and an administrative assistant
- *1971:* Completed construction of the Aritha Spotts Apartments, a 74-unit new construction project costing $1.5 million, including a two-story office and community building (the project was JVL's first development using a HUD rental housing program); also completed seven units of home buyers' housing under a related HUD program

- *Early 1970s:* Persuaded the Model Cities program to invest funds in public improvements in the Martin Luther King shopping district, resulting in improved streets, sidewalks, bus stops, parking, and other public areas
- *1973:* Opened the Aritha Spotts Child Care Center in the Spotts apartment complex, serving 32 children and initially operated with an HEW grant in conjunction with the Early Child Care Development Corporation
- *1974:* Opened the JVL Senior Citizens' Center to house existing programs for the elderly, such as home-delivered meals, with funds from Model Cities, the city of St. Louis (after direct confrontation with the St. Louis Commissioner on Aging and a hearing by the governor) and some HEW funds; also began publication of the neighborhood newspaper *Jeff-Vander-Look*, with the assistance of four students from Washington University
- *1975:* Opened a second day care center at the Bethesda Mennonite Church and in the process effected changes in the state licensing law (a regulation requiring windows in a day care facility was finally waived, allowing for the establishment of the center in the church basement); reorganized the JVL publication into a 12-page monthly newsletter (renamed *JVL News*) published in cooperation with *Proud* magazine; and completed two more HUD 236 rental housing projects, totaling 123 additional units of scattered site rehab housing (according to a JVL report, every housing package proposed through this period was initially rejected by city officials and local and regional HUD staff, with approval coming only after interminable haggling, recalcitrance, and a general attitude of "it will never work"; the report further states that JVL's successes were seldom recognized and then only as exceptions or miracles that could never happen twice)
- *1976:* Began rehabilitation of 98 units (completed in mid-1978) of scattered site housing under a HUD program in conjunction with the National Housing Partnership
- *1977:* Received initial funding for the JVL Communications Center— a $148,000 grant award from the Mott Foundation for renovation, equipment, and program start-up costs—to provide curricula in television, radio, photography, and motion pictures in cooperation with the St. Louis public school system
- *1978:* Currently, JVL is exploring tax-sheltered syndications for further developments in the community, and three more housing packages are in various stages of processing: package #16, 88 units of scattered site infill new construction, already under way; package #17, a 100-unit HUD-supported elderly and handicapped project; and packages #18 and #19, 114 units of rehabilitated and newly constructed units.

12. How did the organization became involved in these activities?

13. How were these activities planned?

14. How were these activities implemented?

15. Have there been difficulties with continued or new funding for these activities?

16. Were different leaders/staff involved in the process of program planning and implementation as contrasted with the founding of the organization?

17. What choices were required, if any, among the various activities?

18. What problems has the organization chosen not to confront?

19. What has been the effect of activities on the organization's basic character over time?

RELATIONSHIP TO VOLUNTARY
ASSOCIATIONS AND NETWORKS

20. Make a list of other organizations or individuals who have voluntarily assisted the organization in a major way.

21. Name three major occasions upon which the target organization has voluntarily assisted other groups.

22. Has the organization ever worked in collaboration with other organizations in the same neighborhood? JVL is especially neighborhood-bound. Housing rehabilitation, child care, and programs for the elderly all have involved joint planning and implementation with the Bethesda Mennonite Church. Mennonite labor and funds went into the earliest housing projects, and one of the JVL child care centers is located in the church.

JVL's "meals on wheels" program for the elderly was created through the joint efforts of JVL and the Yeatman Corporation. This project was first conducted with resources from the Model Cities program and later received St. Louis Area Agency on Aging funding. The JVL Communications

Center, funded in part by the U.S. Department of Labor and the Mott Foundation, is being developed as a neighborhood resource and learning center in collaboration with the St. Louis public school system. Students in the program will spend part of their regular school day at the JVL Communications Center, with 64 youngsters studying such curriculum areas as television, radio, photography, and motion pictures. Their work will include material for the public schools' FM radio station, production of instructional films, creation of a tape library of neighborhood cultural history (stories by elders), and the recording of neighborhood landmarks. For instance, while researching an old school building, several structures (houses) were found to appear on maps indicating that they had been built prior to 1870.

23. Is the organization part of a large umbrella organization? None of the respondents or any of the written material indicated that JVL is formally associated with a large umbrella organization. Through its principal leader, Macler Shepard, JVL is included, however, on many boards and councils. For instance, Shepard is a commissioner on the Bi-State Development Agency, a board member of the Mennonite Mutual Aid, North Side Team Ministry, and United Way, to mention a few such appointments.

24. Is the organization part of a larger citywide, regional, or national network? JVL entered into a joint venture with the National Housing Partnership in 1976, which provided for the financial guarantees required to undertake 98 units of housing. There were no indications that JVL has been a formal member of a network, but through its staff and volunteers, it maintains functional contacts with other development corporations and neighborhood organizations in St. Louis. JVL has worked on specific issues with neighboring communities and tenant organizations in Carr Central, Vaughn, Murphy-Blair, Pruitt-Igoe, and Montgomery-Hyde Park.

25. Describe the relationship between the target organization and other local organizations. JVL has the respect and admiration of other local organizations in terms of its accomplishments in housing developments and other positive projects for the betterment of the JVL area. However, a leader of the Lucas Heights Village housing development summarized the sentiments expressed by other respondents who are associated with the Yeatman Corporation and the Ward 19 alderman. Basically, areas of conflict and competition seemed to surface when discussing what can be accomplished as compared with what only can be dreamed about. Specifically, JVL is thought to be creating an island without adequate ties to other projects like

Lucas Heights located within JVL's borders. Also, JVL depends heavily on HUD funds. These community leaders stated that JVL is very "turf" oriented and is unwilling to change the direction of its development plans to tie into the Lucas Heights project. A political leader expressed what might be considered jealousy among several strong-minded groups. Most respondents thought that the city should assume the role of developing cooperative planning among the several groups.

There were no signs of conflict between JVL and resident groups or the Martin Luther King Business District Association. They have worked together on the market study and several early housing rehabilitation projects.

26. Overall, have outside organizations played an important role in the target organization's life history?

RELATIONSHIP TO CITY GOVERNMENT

27. Does the target organization have any relationship with specific officials or offices in city government? JVL has experienced severe negative relationships with city government in its inception period. Confrontations with city government on bond issues, highway development, industrial park land, code enforcement, Community Development Block Grant uses, and junkyard permits have left a trail of hard feelings and uneasiness between JVL members and city officials.

Relationships with city government, however, persisted and appear to be improving. Macler Shepard maintains a relationship with Mayor Conway and his top aides. Other JVL staff members work with the St. Louis Community Development Agency (CDA) and its executive director, assistant deputy director, and neighborhood planner. Another JVL staff person oversees ties with the St. Louis Agency on Training and Employment (SLATE), which coordinates U.S. Department of Labor funds. Ninth District police officers have been featured in *JVL News* and given special commendation for their efforts to provide better services. There is also a link between JVL and the mayor's office for senior citizens.

In spite of these and other ties to city government, JVL does not hesitate to oppose any action by city government deemed harmful to the JVL area. For example, JVL opposed a bill in early 1977 that would have allowed for certain tax relief for developers, stating that it would bring about neighborhood blight. Further, in 1978, JVL sought action against the St. Louis Board of Adjustment because it supported a junkyard permit, another example of blight according to JVL. JVL will often use the public media and its own *JVL News* to state its case against a government official or agency. Much communication between JVL and city government is formal due to the existence of pressure and confrontation.

The mayor appointed a CDA Citizens' Advisory Committee to receive citizen proposals and municipal agency proposals that are reviewed and rated. The committee's recommendations are given to the city's Neighborhood Betterment Committee and other city departments for review and recommendations. Final approval of proposals is made by the Board of Estimate and Apportionment, the Board of Aldermen, and the mayor. The city's neighborhood planner recommends the selection of the JVL area representative for the advisory committee. The planner makes an independent recommendation and does not seek advice from JVL, Inc.

28. Is the relationship formal or informal?

29. Has this relationship been productive? Mayor Conway indicated that JVL has been able to persuade both federal and private sources to be supportive. He said that the city recognizes JVL's positive contribution and that the city has no quarrels with JVL, generally. However, actions by JVL that have generated conflict were its opposition to both the north-south distributor highway and the rehabilitation of the Cochran Gardens public housing project. With the latter, JVL questioned the St. Louis Housing Authority's plans to rehabilitate one Cochran building at a cost of $3 million, after the authority had opposed a JVL plan to use similar financing mechanisms for four buildings in Pruitt-Igoe at a cost of $5.5 million. The mayor suggested that JVL's actions may have been to gain leverage. However, the mayor noted that the problem has been resolved to some extent and JVL presently has a cooperative relationship with the Housing Authority.

An assistant to Mayor Conway said that the city's relationship with JVL has declined because JVL goes to the media in the middle of negotiations or discussions. He thought that JVL becomes antagonistic rather than seeking advantages. Further, he went on to describe political alliances that have been in opposition to the 19th Ward alderman, creating other sources of conflicts.

Despite the tensions and pressures that characterize the relationship between the city and JVL, the respondent said that JVL housing packages #16 and #18 had recently been placed at the top of the review list, indicating the city's desire to work with JVL. In spite of such tensions, there are signs of a functional and productive relationship. A reporter for the *Globe Democrat* said that Macler Shepard has the respect of city officials.

30. Are there any examples of city government having thwarted the emergence of community organizations? St. Louis currently has many community organizations. The city has established a process of actively assisting such groups. Two requests for proposals (RFPs) have been developed by the CDA—one to develop organizational capacity and the other to fund housing development projects. Also, in early 1977, the CDA formed the St. Louis Local Development Company (LDC) with a $100,000 community development block grant to assist small businesses in obtaining incentive financing.

The city of St. Louis has a neighborhood improvement program funded by a federal $10.1 million public works grant. The grant is administered by the CDA. The primary emphasis is on street and parks improvements. JVL is included in this program, as it is focusing on those areas with extensive private housing rehabilitation.

31. Has the city made any structural changes in its own organization to be more supportive and competent with respect to neighborhood preservation and revitalization goals generally? CDA was reorganized two years ago. The reorganization resulted in the establishment of 18 planning districts as a citywide basis for neighborhood planning. Seven neighborhood planners are assigned to the 18 districts. Their role is to assess the districts' priority needs. The planners dialogue with neighborhood representatives and conduct field inspections. The planners are expected to consult with neighborhood leaders, and the plans emanating from this process guide block grant improvements in the neighborhoods.

The neighborhood planner who works with JVL indicated that the city did not provide site improvement funds to assist neighborhood improvement projects until 1977. The planner noted that it happened as a result of public demand.

32. What are the target organization's main relationships outside the city?

33. Overall, has the city government played an important role in the target organization's life history?

OUTCOMES

Condition of the Neighborhood

34. During the lifetime of the organization, has there been any tangible evidence of neighborhood improvement? Neighborhood improvement in the JVL area surveyed over its lifetime is significant, visible, and dramatic. Even those respondents whose views were critical of JVL's methods and plans clearly acknowledged its accomplishments. Housing development, both new and rehabilitated, is the foremost achievement of JVL. Housing units are developed in what is referred to as a "package" assembled by technical experts, including architects, general contractors, lending institution executives, insurance agents, and others, under the guidance of the JVL staff and board of directors. To date, 18 packages have been developed, containing a total of 623 units of new or rehabilitated housing. The packages have ranged in size from 4 to 100 units. Months of detailed work and negotiations are devoted to the creation and development of these packages.

The writer observed many of the improvements during several tours of the JVL neighborhood. Capital improvement, with the exception of dwelling units, was not as evident. In the early 1970s, JVL advocated the use of Model Cities funds to improve the Martin Luther King shopping district. Improvements such as street paving, new sidewalks, tree planting, bus stops, and off-street parking were undertaken at a cost of several hundred thousand dollars, according to a JVL report. In 1976, the *JVL News* reported that the area suffered from neglect and poor maintenance. The plaza still lacks proper upkeep. JVL has included further developments in the area as part of its economic reinvestment plan. According to the *JVL News*, the target organization has been responsible for getting the Metropolitan Sewer District to give more and better service to the area.

This writer observed that sidewalks and curbs are greatly deteriorated throughout the area. Vacant lots are trash-ridden and overgrown with high weeds. JVL puts continuous pressure on city departments to combat such problems. The *JVL News* is used effectively to criticize when nothing is done and to announce results as they occur. Currently, much of JVL's efforts is focused on sidewalk improvements and construction of infill housing—new housing units on vacant lots.

In 1968, JVL influenced the Brown Shoe Company to build a shoe factory in the neighborhood. The factory provides 300 to 450 jobs. In the November 1976 edition of *JVL News*, the plant supervisor reported a 97% attendance record. Brown Shoe also has a training program for both foremen and supervisors. JVL maintains a personnel office to screen and test applicants for jobs. In terms of law enforcement, JVL summarizes resident complaints and has periodically identified the current "hot spot"—a corner or street that is then highlighted in the *JVL News* and reported to the police. Any subsequent improvements also are reported.

35. Has there been any evidence of the organization having blocked or prevented some change in the physical condition of the neighborhood?

Residents' Perceptions

36. What do residents feel about the target organization? Many respondents noted that the activities and accomplishments of JVL have contributed to the significant decrease in every category of crime between 1970 and 1976. The decrease is evidenced by police statistics contained in the 1977 market study.

According to a reporter from the *Globe Democrat*, the JVL neighborhood lacks stores, shops, and cultural events and institutions of the type that would attract young, middle-income persons into the neighborhood, with the exception of those committed to repopulating the North Side and those believing in self-help in the black community. He said that such persons also would be willing to take more risks—referring to a widespread belief that the JVL area is unsafe, despite the reported decrease in crime. The reporter does not live in the JVL area, but his reporting assignments include JVL.

A resident whose comments summarized the sentiments of a number of persons living in the JVL neighborhood said that, to him, the neighborhood is like a frontier. He noted that the people who own their homes take better care of them. He indicated that the basics for power (unity of the people in an organized effort) are in the JVL neighborhood. Residents felt positive about JVL, most often citing the physical improvements in housing and the continuous advocacy role played by JVL on behalf of the area. Several respondents described easy access to participation and involvement. For example, one resident went to a monthly meeting to hear about plans to improve vacant lots. He presented an idea, and city bulldozers arrived within 10 days. The resident now keeps the lot clean.

37. Do residents feel that the target organization has addressed the neighborhood's problems? All the residents interviewed felt that JVL has addressed the most significant area problems. Commercial development as well as general maintenance and cleanup are problems that were most often mentioned. Commercial reinvestment is anticipated based on the completion of the Martin Luther King Business District market study. Most respondents believe that JVL is presently working near its capacity, so that commercial ventures must be delayed until new funding sources and other resources are obtained. Problems of inadequate city services have been attributed to the belief that the city has (until recently) attempted to eliminate sections of the North Side community to allow for the development of an industrial park and new highway construction.

38. Have the activities of the target organization resulted in increased residential activity? JVL activities for older adults have generated new and varied services for many elderly. Films, speakers, transportation and escort service, shopping assistance, and welfare problem assistance bring together hundreds of elderly persons weekly. Teens and young adults have greater access to both recreational and educational activities as a result of the Summer Youth Program. The summer activities of the young people focused on the neighborhood. For instance, a visual arts project on display showed their own concepts for a new recreational facility. Also, a film produced by the youth featured familiar locations in the area. The awards ceremony was filled to capacity with persons of all ages from the JVL neighborhood.

JVL holds monthly community meetings at the Mennonite Church. Respondents stated that the attendance fluctuates, based on the interest in the topics being discussed. The topics have included tax increases (with top city officials present), vacant lot programs, health issues such as alcoholism and sales tax on medicines, the election of JVL's board of trustees, as well as JVL's program plans. JVL residents contact city officials through formal meetings, telephone, and other direct interaction in part because JVL discloses the identities of the city officials directly responsible for various services. JVL publishes a telephone guide in the *JVL News* that gets heavy use, according to respondents. The guide includes many city hall telephone numbers.

According to JVL's leaders, JVL works with many block clubs and their parent organization, the Federation of Block Units. However, there has been no indication of JVL having created additional clubs. Several organizations such as the Congress of Neighborhood Organizations in North St. Louis and the North Side Team Ministry include some JVL leadership. The congress has helped to air issues through press conferences and information gathering. It has dealt with issues such as social services, housing, neighborhood betterment, citizen participation, programs for low- and moderate-income families, and the distribution of government funds. The ministry serves as a weekly outreach and community feedback channel for JVL, as well as for the clergy.

39. Are there any specific instances of a resident having become more influential outside the neighborhood because of the target organization?

40. Is there increased unity or fragmentation in the neighborhood since the founding of the organization? JVL's contribution to neighborhood unity seems to border on the spiritual. Macler Shepard at times appears to be a preacher and the neighborhood his congregation. The respect that he appears to enjoy is reinforced by a warm admiration felt for him by persons throughout the neighborhood. Shepard himself is certainly among the unifying factors in the JVL neighborhood. JVL has a reputation for being, in one word, "tenacious," according to respondents (including Mayor Conway and other city officials).

Race and Social Justice

41. How has the organization dealt with neighborhood problems of race and poverty? JVL's entire roster of activities has related to the plight of poor and black people. Its record of accomplishments is evidence of activities designed to deal with the problems of being poor and black in a large and older American city. This whole case study is a response to the issues of race and poverty.

42. How has the target organization responded to patterns of neighborhood transition—that is, displacement, integration, and resegregation? JVL has attempted to retain older residents through the development of new subsidized housing for the elderly. In other cases, JVL has sold property back to renters under highly favorable terms, after renovation. JVL has sought to rehabilitate older, but sound, structures for habitation by persons in the middle- and upper-income levels. There is a clear pattern of economic integration under way in the JVL housing development program.

According to respondents who are white, there is no racial integration occurring in the JVL neighborhood. Although they live and work at a church in the area, they have broad contacts through the neighborhood. Prospects of racial integration may be related only to a school desegregation case that has been in the courts for several years. No other prospects seem imminent. The business community in the JVL area is integrated and works cooperatively with the organization. The JVL workforce also is integrated.

43. Have problems of race or ethnic division arisen in the target organization? Leaders and other respondents indicated that such divisions have not arisen. The unique team that provided the initial leadership for JVL was comprised of black and white as well as female and male persons. Leadership and support workforce members share similar diversity today. Problems that were mentioned related to personality differences.

44. Over time, have there been any changes in the organization's policies or activities with regard to any of the issues in the preceding four questions?

45. How do the organization's leaders or members describe the accomplishments and disappointments from JVL's activities? [A list of 22 principal accomplishments appeared in the original case study, most of them already covered in earlier responses.]

The following are the principal disappointments:

- Demolition of the Pruitt-Igoe public housing complex and, in particular, the four buildings in the complex that JVL proposed to rehabilitate and manage
- Demolition of other landmarks, such as the Divoll School, built in 1872
- Rejection of the Opportunity House funding request by the United Way of Greater St. Louis
- Failure to cause the city to take action against illegal junkyards and other blight scattered throughout the JVL area
- Failure to win local government support for large-scale funding of public improvements to enhance housing developments

46. How has the organization enhanced community leadership or increased the involvement of residents?

47. Does the organization have a capability of dealing with multiple issues simultaneously?

48. During the lifetime of the organization, what situations, if any, threatened the survival of the organization? The principal threat to JVL's survival over its lifetime has been the need to raise money to survive, according to its leaders. JVL has dealt with that threat by continuously developing new funding sources and structuring the organization's fiscal practices along the lines of business and industry, striving for increased levels of self-generated or self-controlled revenues for a $200,000 core budget.

Other threats have come from the constant battle with local government. JVL has a history of confronting local political issues directly and mobilizing its base of support and respect in the JVL neighborhood, according to both JVL writings and respondents.

49. Are there any specific incidents that best characterize the work of the organization? Macler Shepard claims that "we dedicated ourselves to the community," and words such as "inspiration" and "dedication" characterize much of the JVL spirit. One young adult respondent who plans to reside in the JVL area said that she wants "to build equity in the neighborhood and realize a return from it—not money, but the sense of satisfaction that comes when you go home in the evening and say, I've accomplished something— whether it's picking up trash or responding to the questions of young people who involve themselves at the (Communications Resources) Center."

LIST OF RESPONDENTS
AND ANNOTATED BIBLIOGRAPHY

[The original case study lists 25 persons, with detailed titles, addresses, and telephone numbers, as well as complete references to 34 documents, reports, and printed materials.]

3

Computer Implementation in a Local School System

Schools have successfully used computers to advance teaching and learning. The present case comes from an earlier era, when schools were first implementing personal computers (then called "microcomputers"). The case (1 of 12 in the original study) describes the computer applications undertaken by a school district and the organizational conditions believed to be associated with successful implementation.

The data for the 12 cases were collected by using a common case study protocol (see Boxes 8 and 9). As a result, the composition of all 12 cases also follows the same outline—first, a description of the computer systems and applications, and second, a review of four organizational issues representing the main hypotheses of interest for cross-case analysis. In addition, the case draws attention to special education because the original case studies were commissioned to examine computer use in special education.

Given this overall design, each individual case study illustrates a descriptive case. Key methodological features in the case are the attention to chronological sequences and the use of vignettes to describe qualitative, embedded units of analysis within the broader case. The original case study has been edited for readability, mainly by replacing the term "microcomputer" with the more commonly understood "personal computer" or "PC." However, the references to specific types of hardware have been retained, to give the reader a flavor of the PC world's early days.

AUTHOR'S NOTE: This case study appears as Appendix B in a report titled *Microcomputer Implementation in Schools* (COSMOS Corporation, March 1984) by Robert K. Yin and J. Lynne White. The report covers a multiple-case analysis of 12 case studies. Five of the individual cases, including the present case, were produced as appendices. In the interest of making the case more readable, the original case study has been edited lightly and a table has been omitted. The cross-case analysis appeared later in Yin and White, 1985.

BOX 8

The Importance of a Case Study Protocol and Common Preparation and Training When Doing a Case Study

The case study in this chapter was 1 of 12 conducted by *multiple investigators* serving on the same research team, each doing a subset of the cases in a multiple-case study. Under these circumstances, having a common case study protocol and common preparation were essential.

Unlike the situation where a *solo investigator* may be doing an entire case study, the team members must ensure that they will use parallel procedures and methods. Otherwise, the resulting multiple-case study will produce uneven results, with variations introduced by case study team members wrongly being accepted as variations in the component cases.

The role of protocols and formal preparation may be less important if a single investigator is doing an entire case study. However, the single investigator must still be concerned about unwanted variations in data collection procedures, either from case to case when doing a multiple-case study or from time period to time period when doing a single-case study. As a general precaution, a case study protocol may still be desirable, even for solo investigations.

(For more information, see Yin, 2003, Chapter 3, section on "Training and Preparation for a Specific Case Study.")

THE COMPUTER SYSTEM IN OPERATION

The School District

Minuteman Regional Vocational Technical School District is a one-school vocational and technical education district established in 1975 by agreement of 16 neighboring towns. The school is located on 65 acres of woods and fields in Lexington and Lincoln, Massachusetts, 10 miles west of Boston. Admission to the school is open to any student within its member towns and serves as an option to the local high schools. As a one-school district, the school building contains both district staff (headed by a superintendent) and school staff (headed by a principal), although the two staffs work closely together.

The vocational-technical programs are organized into nine clusters: building trades, commercial services, electronics, graphics, health services, metal fabrication, power mechanics, distributive education/child care, and

---

BOX 9

**Case Study Protocols: Aimed at the
Investigator, Not Interviewees**

Because most social science instruments contain questions for interviewees (if not respondents), a frequent misconception is that a case study protocol has the same property. However, the case study protocol is in fact entirely different. It itemizes questions or issues to be addressed by the case study investigator and describes the field procedures to be followed, serving as the investigator's field agenda. The coauthors of the present case followed just such a protocol.

You can address the protocol's questions by obtaining data from any source—that is, by reviewing documents, making direct observations, or conducting interviews. Because the protocol is the agenda for the data collection, the topics in a good protocol also can serve as the outline for the case study report, as in the present case study.

(For more information, see Yin, 2003, Chapter 3, section on "The Case Study Protocol.")

---

technology. Each cluster represents several departments focusing on a particular trade or skill area, with required courses for each grade level. Students gain practical experience in their vocational area through the shops and services operated by the school for the public, such as a restaurant, bakery, beauty salon, service station, child care center, and landscaping service. The academic areas covered are English, mathematics, science, social studies, business, foreign languages, physical education, and a few electives.

The school program operates on a "week about" schedule, in which one full week is spent in academic subjects and the following week in a lab or shop. Thus, academic and vocational weeks are alternated throughout the school year. Currently, 1,252 students attend Grades 9 to 12, each earning a high school diploma and a technical certificate in one of 25 occupational areas.

Special education services are provided to 450 of these students. The special education program is largely intermingled with the vocational and academic programs, because the students admitted to the school must possess prevocational and academic skills. The special education students are assigned to resource teachers for educational support and guidance, using at least one academic period a day. More time may be spent in the resource room, depending on a student's skill levels and ability to take the regular academic subjects. In addition, special education students with poor reading and math skills are assigned to developmental labs for remedial work.

Computer Systems in the District

Minuteman has a total of 27 personal computers (PCs), of which 22 are Apple II-Plus units and 5 are Zenith Heathkit models. In addition, the school has three Digital PDP-11 minicomputers with terminals for both administrative and instructional functions, and there are two additional Apple II-Plus units in a regional resource center for teachers, located in the Minuteman building but organizationally independent of the district. The district's computer center (an administrative unit) administers the three Digital PDP-11 minicomputers, which replaced two minicomputers that had been in operation through 1981-1982. In addition to the computer center, terminals to the minicomputers are located in the data processing department (a computer lab for students) and in the special education, guidance, nurse's, and dean's offices, serving the three major functions noted below.

• *Instructional use*: Students in the data processing department of the electronic cluster have full use of one minicomputer and its terminals, in conjunction with their computer lab (for programming and technician training).
• *Student information*: All of the district's attendance, grade reports, warning lists, student medical information, student information system, special education student data, special education quarterly reports, and class scheduling are done by the minicomputers.
• *Administration*: The payroll, accounts payable, budget, and related records (including service to the Town of Lincoln) are done by the minicomputers.

The Target System

The target system for this case study consisted of the 22 Apple II-Plus PCs at the school. Most of the units have color monitors and several have double disk drives. There are eight dot matrix printers and one printer of letter quality. A few of the PCs are equipped with a graphic drawing tablet, a light pen, or joysticks for special applications. The system also has recently been augmented by a hard disk drive for a future software project, as well as a system for interactive, videocassette display.

Location. Of these 22 PCs, 14 are located in offices or individual classrooms and 8 are in a computer center in the library. Each of six vocational areas—culinary arts, machine shop, carpentry, electronics, distributive education, and instrumentation—has a PC located in its work space. The English department has one unit placed in a small workroom. In the science department, one computer is moved around to different classrooms. There is one PC in the developmental math lab. The guidance office has one unit, and the superintendent has a unit in his office. The computer coordinating office, which also functions as a resource room, has three PCs and one printer. Finally, eight of the PCs and two printers are in the computer center, which is a section of the library/media center, and to which teachers can send their students for computer use during class time. With its eight PCs, the center serves students from all the resource rooms in addition to the overflow from several departments, including math, carpentry, English, and electronics.

Applications. The PCs are used for a wide variety of applications, mostly instructional rather than administrative, with over 100 pieces of software integrated into the curriculum. The following are examples of these instructional uses:

- Special education offers individualized instruction in basic skills, computer literacy, and other areas that contribute to academic learning, visual perception, and decision making (see Vignette 1).

- In science, computer programs are used for tutorial instruction in chemistry, biology, and physics (see Vignette 2).

- Electronics students learn to write BASIC and Pascal programs and also receive computer-assisted instruction (CAI) in math. Some students are learning to use database management software, while others create games using graphics.

- The computer center provides basic skill instruction to any student on subjects such as math, spelling, grammar, reading, and social studies. The computers also are used to train all freshmen on computer use and some seniors in basic programming.

- The culinary arts department uses a computer to operate a daily, shop-inventory control program for the student-run bakery.

- A special vocational project, "Super Insulated House," is under way, combining the student expertise of the instrumentation department in using the computers for environmental monitoring and control with the skills of the building trades department for construction.

VIGNETTE 1

Individualized Instruction: Special Education

In this application, three students at a time work in the computer coordinating office, which also serves as a resource room for special education students. Along two sides of the small room are three PCs with one printer. A metal file cabinet contains a selection of software.

One student may work on a math program of word problems that uses a gamelike format. The emphasis is on whole-number operations as well as reading skills. The teacher indicates that the program is typical of most of the math drill-and-practice software used in building basic skills. Another student may have recently become interested in PCs and is learning the basic elements of programming. These students are part of a program for special education students that provides individualized instruction on PCs, with an additional emphasis on computer literacy. Students are selected for the program based on their resource teachers' recommendations and the learning objectives contained in their Individual Education Plans (IEPs). The program is taught by the computer master teacher who also acts as a resource teacher for special education students.

The computer master teacher says that at the beginning of his course, none of the students could even operate a PC. After he works with each of the 20 to 30 students for approximately 40 minutes (for 8 weeks), the students can use software independently, and most of them can write simple programs. In accordance with the students' IEPs, they use drill-and-practice programs, strategic games, and simulations to help develop academic skills, visual perception, and decision-making strategies.

In addition, the school's staff has developed computer-based lessons in spelling, vocabulary, literature, and history, to assist students in their academic courses.

Administrative uses of the computers include the following:

- Capital inventory control for each department
- Staff attendance records
- Student test data records (see Vignette 3)
- Some word processing

Finally, the superintendent uses his PC for financial planning and simulations of contract negotiations. The PC also provides data and graphics for the superintendent's work with public hearings and finance committees.

VIGNETTE 2

Computer-Assisted Instruction in Science

In this application, each planet is slowly drawn on the screen in a colorful display. The orbits of the planets and the comets, as well as the planets' sizes in relation to the other heavenly bodies, also are brilliantly animated. This program is a minimovie about the solar system, in which the student is given information about individual planets and their moons, comets and asteroids, and other illustrations of complex orbital relationships.

Students usually work individually at the PCs with a software program that corresponds to the material presented in class. The teachers first use this program as a demonstration to the entire class. The science department's single PC is on wheels and can be moved from one classroom to the next. It is used at the front of the room for the entire classroom and moved into a quiet corner for individual use. Only the interested students continue using the program, once it has been demonstrated for both practice and reinforcement. The science teacher is adamant about no one being forced to use the PC. However, some students who are absent or behind in their work are urged to use it.

The science teacher says that the PC is popular with most of the students and can be found in daily use in the basic science class for special education students. Fifteen students attend the science class for a double period, so each student can use the PC at least once a week for approximately 20 minutes.

Regarding the overall level of use, only estimates exist. It is believed that 80 of the 130 vocational and academic teachers use the PCs on a regular basis. Of the 10 resource teachers (special education), six are said to use the PCs with their students in the computer coordinating office or the computer center. Among district personnel, the superintendent is the only user, and none of the school administrators uses PCs in their work.

According to the computer master teacher, approximately half the students (about 600) use the PCs on a regular basis in connection with their shop skills or academic learning. It is estimated that at least 50% (300) of these users are special education students. Furthermore, all freshmen students are given introductory training in computer literacy. In terms of use, the computer center, for example, averages 70 or more students per day. The computer specialist in charge says that it is rare to have a PC available in the center during any period in a given day. As another example, the PC in the developmental math lab is used by 140 special education students for 40 minutes each, once a week. Each department with a PC has a similar schedule that suggests constant use.

VIGNETTE 3

Recordkeeping System

In this application, an English teacher interested in the administrative uses of the PC has developed a recordkeeping system for the entire department. An existing computer program was adapted to code the various test scores pertinent to the curriculum.

The English teacher was responsible for the initial data entry on all students in the fall of 1982. Once the system was established, she taught the other four English teachers to enter and retrieve information. The actual records are used in a number of ways. Teachers can enter student ID numbers and receive a listing of each student's test scores and grades. Lists of students who have completed competency requirements can be searched and printed. The system also can identify students who lack a specific skill or need certain courses to complete their curriculum.

This system replaces manual files on each student kept by different teachers, which were not coordinated and demanded unnecessary duplication. It is the first attempt at maintaining a central information file on testing in the school and is expected to be adopted by the math department next year. Once a year, the records are printed, with the data disks being updated throughout the school year. The printing has created some problems because the English department's PC is not equipped with a printer, and time has to be scheduled on the printers in the computer center and office. It is expected that a printer will soon be purchased because it is a major part of the application.

Compared to this more intense instructional use, the level of administrative use has been low but growing, in part due to changes in the minicomputer system. Originally, the minicomputer staff in the computer center had little or nothing to do with the PC system. However, the large and diverse minicomputer applications have created constant overloading of the minicomputer system, especially because it relies on disk drives of limited capacity. As a result, the system has frequent downtime. This problem was not as severe in previous years, because the disk drives in the older system had (paradoxically) a larger capacity.

The problem of downtime, coupled with tight schedules for access time, has led some minicomputer users to develop a preference for the PCs. For example, the guidance office now uses a PC in addition to its minicomputer terminal, for easier and more flexible management of certain student data and attendance records. These uses have led the computer master teacher to note, "The computer center, along with the data processing department, has realized—but only in the last few months—that the PCs are a power to be used."

Management of the Personal Computers

The superintendent makes all final decisions about computer purchases and budgets, with approval from the school board. These purchasing decisions are made in conjunction with the computer master teacher, who was previously a resource teacher in the developmental math lab. This teacher now divides his time about equally between his special education responsibilities and coordinating the PC activities in the school, and he is responsible for providing in-service training, maintaining the equipment, and serving as a continuing resource to the staff members and students.

This master teacher is part of the special education staff and has no formal organizational relationship to the vocational education staff. However, the master teacher acts in an informal manner to assure that all of the target system's needs are satisfied. For instance, he prepares annual estimates for new or upgraded units, based on his experience.

In the computer center, a relevant staff person is the computer specialist, whose responsibilities include scheduling and managing the use of the center's PCs and maintaining the district's software library. The computer specialist also provides general computer literacy as well as independent computer projects to any interested student.

Decisions to purchase computer software are made in a collaborative manner. Because the software purchases are made from existing library and departmental budgets for materials, individual teachers may suggest the software to be purchased. These suggestions may then be reviewed by the computer specialist, by the various departments, or by the computer master teacher before a purchase decision is made. Maintenance decisions are made by the superintendent and the computer master teacher. In 1982-1983, a general maintenance contract was discontinued (due to high cost), and the master teacher now personally performs any necessary maintenance.

Chronology

The superintendent had first brought the idea of PC use into the school at the beginning of 1980. The impetus was a visit to California in December 1979. He viewed the new technology as an invaluable teaching tool that "successfully combined patience with interactive learning." He posted a note to solicit the interest of other teachers. Within several weeks, a committee of staff members was formed to investigate the use of PCs at other schools and to make recommendations for purchasing hardware.

By the late fall of 1980, 10 Apple II-Plus PCs and software and one TRS-80 and two printers had been purchased, primarily with Occupational Education Entitlement funds (P.L. 94-482). An additional unit was purchased in the spring of 1981. The first PCs were allocated to the staff members who had shown the most interest and were likely to have success with implementation. However, the innovation was not mandated by the superintendent, nor were any departments pressured to adopt PCs. He wanted students to experience computers in the context of their vocational or technical area and not just in a center or in a reading or a math department. In September of 1981, the superintendent, in consultation with the computer master teacher, purchased nine additional Apple II-Plus PCs and printers. The computer center expanded to accommodate seven units. In the 1982 academic year, another Apple-II Plus was acquired, and all units were upgraded to 64K. A hard disk drive and additional hardware also were added. Decisions on the distribution of the new units again were made on the basis of a teacher demonstrating an ability to use the machine for either instructional or administrative purposes. A written plan for use was considered inadequate; the acceptable demonstration of need consisted of running programs in the resource center, writing new software, or testing new applications for others. Insufficient use of a unit has been grounds for having a computer removed, which has occurred once. The superintendent's attitude and involvement continues to be one of "I will provide the means to support the use of computers, if you prove how to make use of them." In addition, several teachers were given the opportunity to develop their own programs over the summer.

As an extension of the training (see below), six of the most interested and proficient in-service graduates were paid during the summer of 1981 to develop instructional software in their academic or trade areas. These efforts resulted in a vocational aptitude evaluation package for the guidance office, computer-assisted instruction programs for the distributive education and culinary arts department, and software on grammar and sentence construction for the English students. The school's software collection, purchased with library funds, was indexed and catalogued in the fall of 1981 for a printed *Personal Computer Program Guide*.

The position of computer master teacher was created by the superintendent to act as a resource to the new users. When the center was expanded,

Table 3.1

Chronology of Implementation: Minuteman School District

Date	Event
January 1980	Committee of interested persons formed to recommend hardware
June 1980	Purchase of one TRS-80 and one Apple II-Plus and software
September 1980	Position of PC master teacher established
October 1980	First teacher training offered (15 hours)
November 1980	Purchase of nine Apple II-Plus units and two printers; designed and built two workstations
April 1981	Purchase of one Apple II-Plus
June 1981	Five teachers paid over summer to develop software programs
September 1981	Half-time position of PC master teacher created
September 1981	Purchase of nine Apple II-Plus units and printers
September 1981	Set up PC center with four Apples; position of PC specialist for center established
September-November 1981	More training
November 1981	Printed PC guide B-14
September 1982	Purchase of one Apple II-Plus and upgrading of all PCs to 64K
September 1982	Formalized computer coordination program for all freshmen
September 1982	Purchase of Corvus hard disk drive
November 1982	Purchase of Cavri system and two videocassettes
November 1982	Formed micro/minicomputer coordination committee

a teacher was assigned the position of computer specialist to manage the center's activities.

The first computer in-service training took place in the fall of 1980, after the school's purchase of the first 10 PCs. The course was open to all staff members and ran for 2 hours, once a week after school, for 15 weeks. Under the tutelage of the superintendent and with assistance from the computer master teacher and the hardware supplier, 60 teachers learned the rudiments of PC use. The course covered system operation, the evaluation and selection of software, and classroom lesson development. Additional in-service training has been provided by the computer master teacher, to meet the growing interests and needs of the staff. Other activities have included a formal computer orientation for freshmen and the formation of a PC coordination committee.

ORGANIZATIONAL ISSUES

Centralization and Decentralization

The PC system at Minuteman exemplifies both centralized and decentralized approaches, occurring simultaneously by design. The superintendent and computer master teacher have—on the one hand—exercised strong, central control in determining computer acquisition and assignment patterns. This has included decisions on acquiring new units each year, on the upgrading of existing units, and on the maintenance of the school's software catalog. In addition, the centralized control has led to the location of some of the computer units in centralized places—for example, the media center.

On the other hand, some PCs are assigned to individual classrooms, and this leads to decentralized control because the teachers are able to use the computers as they see fit. Initially, the teachers do not simply receive the computers but must first demonstrate their ability to use and integrate the them into the ongoing classroom plans. Once demonstrated, the computers are assigned to their classrooms, but if subsequent underuse occurs, the unit may be reassigned to some other location.

Outside the target computer system, other hardware decisions can be made independently of the computer master teacher. This occurred recently when the vocational education staff acquired five Heathkit PCs for its electronics cluster—without consulting the master teacher, but with the superintendent's final approval. Similarly, decisions regarding the IBM minicomputers have been made independently of the considerations for the target PC system.

Interaction Between Special and Regular Education

Minuteman is a vocational-technical school, and there is relatively little distinction between the special and regular education services. Special education students are mainstreamed into the entire program but at the same time are given specialized staff assistance in the form of work in resource rooms. Overall, however, these distinctions have not led to any clear differences regarding the use of PCs for special education as opposed to vocational education. One feature worth reiterating is that the computers have largely been purchased with non–special education (i.e., Occupational Education Entitlement) funds.

Interaction Between Administrative and Instructional Applications

This is not a major issue, even though a few administrative applications exist. In general, the PCs are dedicated to instructional applications, with the administrative uses having only recently emerged. The single major exception is the one PC assigned to the superintendent, who uses it for administrative purposes. (The dominance of the instructional applications was one reason for selecting this site in the first place.) In general, computer resources outside the target PC are used for administrative applications. Increasing attention has been given to the coordination between the PCs and these other systems. For instance, a need arose this year to coordinate the acquisition of new equipment, such as a printer, that in principle could be compatible with both systems. Such needs have resulted in some further collaborative efforts—for example, the formation of a "coordinating committee" by the computer master teacher and computer center director.

Personnel Resources

Training. Training currently takes place on a regular basis through minicourses conducted every 5 weeks after school for 2-hour sessions. Each course is a basic introduction of the use of PCs, including instructional and administrative applications. As an example of the typical attendance for these courses, 50 staff members completed the two courses offered in the fall of 1982. The master teacher's PC office also is used for training on a continual, informal basis. Teachers request time with the master teacher during free periods or after school, to learn anything from simple computer operations to basic programming.

Emerging Roles. To assist the initiation of PC use in the district, the superintendent created two new roles in the fall of 1981. First, the superintendent assigned one teacher the responsibility of being the computer master teacher. Second, a staff person in the media center/library became the computer specialist in the computer center. The specialist's main responsibility includes scheduling and managing the use of the center's PCs as well as maintaining the district's software library. The specialist also provides general computer literacy as well as independent computer projects to any interested student. In addition to his regular school hour functions, the specialist also teaches adult education evening classes in computer literacy and a PC summer camp at the school.

REFERENCES

[The original case study identified 17 persons by name, along with their titles at the time of the case study. The case study also cited 32 documents, including publications, forms, manuals, and other school materials used in conducting the case study.]

PART III

Explanatory Case Studies

4

A Nutshell Example: The Effect of a Federal Award on a University Computer Science Department

Explanatory case studies are the most difficult and the most frequently challenged. Each case study seeks to explain how and why some event(s) occurred. Embedded in the explanation is a potential causal path, whereby a case study seems to be making an inroad into the attribution problem.

Can case studies, especially single-case studies, prove anything? The answer is, "Not with the certainty of true experiments." However, the following example shows how the case can still suggest important clues to possible cause-and-effect relationships. In the absence of the ability to conduct true experiments, such clues may be the best that can be attained, and doing an explanatory case study may be better than not making any inquiry at all.

The illustrative example was not originally a case study. Rather, the example comes from an abstract to the final report of a research grant written by its principal investigator. The writer attempts to attribute significant organizational changes (in a university computer science department) to the use of funds from a federal grant. Serendipitously, the abstract's logic contains the essential ingredients of an explanatory case study. Because of its one-page length, the abstract does not contain sufficient data or evidence to support its logic. However, the essence of the logic serves as an excellent point of departure for understanding how to develop an explanatory case study.

To demonstrate the usefulness of the logic, the present author has added methodological commentary (see bracketed items) to the original text written by the original principal investigator.

AUTHOR'S NOTE: This chapter is based on a one-page abstract from a final grant report for Award No. DCR81-05763 from the National Science Foundation (NSF) to Cornell University, covering the period from June 1, 1981, to November 30, 1986. The abstract was written by the principal investigator of the grant, David Gries, and is dated February 27, 1987. The abstract is presented in its original form, with methodological comments added.

From 1980 to 1986, the Computer Science Department at Cornell was radically transformed from a theoretical, pencil-and-paper research operation to one with a high degree of experimental computing. The departmental computing facility grew from a VAX/780 and a PDP11/60 to an integrated complex of almost 100 workstations and UNIX mainframes. All faculty and graduate students now use computing daily **[a sequentially earlier outcome, further itemized below]**, and much research that was hitherto impossible for us is now being performed **[a sequentially later outcome, operationalized further below]**.

The change in emphasis was due to the maturing of computer science **[a concurrent condition that also can be a rival explanation]**, to commensurate changes in the interests of the faculty **[another concurrent condition]**, and to hardware and software advances that made flexible computing available at an affordable price **[a third concurrent condition]**. However, without the NSF's five-year CER (Coordinated Experimental Research) grant DCR81-05763, it would not have been possible **[main hypothesized intervention]**. The CER grant provided the wherewithal that allowed the department to change with the times; it provided equipment and maintenance, gave us leverage with vendors for acquiring other equipment, and funded staffing of the faculty **[critical how-and-why explanation for how the intervention worked to produce the outcomes observed next]**.

The influence of the grant can be seen by mentioning just a few of the more important projects that it has stimulated. Turing Award winner John Hopcroft changed his interests from the theory of algorithms and computational complexity to robotics and now heads a growing and forceful group that is experimenting with robotics and solid modeling **[operationalized outcome]**. Theoretician Robert Constable and his group have been developing a system for "mechanizing" mathematics. This system, which has inspired many theoretical as well as experimental advances, has as one of its goals the extraction of a program from a mathematical proof; it gives a glimpse into how professional programming might be done 20 years from now **[a second operationalized outcome]**. Tim Teitelbaum and his group generalized his work on the well-known Program Synthesizer into a system that is able to generate such a programming environment from a formal description of a language; the resulting Synthesizer Generator has been released to over 120 sites worldwide **[a third]**. Ken Birman's group is developing an experimental distributed operating system for dealing with fault tolerance **[a fourth]**. And visitor Paul Pritchard used the facility for his work on prime numbers, resulting in the first known arithmetic progression of nineteen primes **[a fifth]**.

The CER grant enabled the department to attract bright young faculty who would not have joined a department with inadequate facilities **[yet another outcome]**. As a result, the department has been able to branch out into new areas, such as VLSI, parallel architectures and code optimization, functional programming, and artificial intelligence **[a second]**. The CER program did what it set out to do: it made it possible for the department to expand its research activity, making it far more experimental and computing intensive while still maintaining strong theoretical foundations **[general outcome]**.

5

Essential Ingredients of Explanatory Case Studies

Three Drug Prevention Examples

These three illustrative cases were developed specifically for case study training purposes. To this end, the text contains special markings. First, the key evidence in the text has been italicized. Second, the topics listed in the righthand column represent the presumed line of explanatory argument being made by the case.

The cases were deliberately written in an abbreviated manner to show the essential logic underlying explanatory case studies. The basic claim underlying each case is that (1) a community formed (2) a partnership that in turn supported (3) activities leading to (4) reductions in substance abuse. Arraying data to present these presumed cause-and-effect links is the main challenge of each abbreviated case study.

The abbreviated versions are based on an original set of case studies that were much more extensive and contained greater detail and additional evidence. The lengthier cases are clearly stronger, providing more evidence, but the purpose of the abbreviated versions is to illustrate the essential explanatory logic, not to provide detailed evidence.

A key feature in the design of the cases is that none is accompanied by any comparison cases. On the contrary, the illustrative cases

AUTHOR'S NOTE: This chapter contains highly condensed versions of case study reports completed by COSMOS Corporation for the Center for Substance Abuse Prevention, Substance Abuse and Mental Health Services Administration, U.S. Department of Health and Human Services. The original reports and the condensed versions were written by staff members of COSMOS under the supervision of Robert K. Yin, who was the project director for the entire effort. The condensed versions, with fictionalized community names, were produced specifically for the purpose of illustrating explanatory case studies and were not part of the original effort. They have been successfully used in numerous case study training sessions and have been edited for inclusion in this chapter.

assume that, as in many community studies, the identification of a comparison case is precluded by either resource or definitional constraints. Instead, the cases illustrate the use of rival explanations, in part to compensate for the absence of a comparison case. Some rivals deal with the newness and distinctiveness of the partnership; others with whether the partnership in fact was the main instigator of the critical activities; and finally, yet others with the link between the activities and drug prevention outcomes. The more that such rival explanations are identified and rejected, the stronger the resulting causal reasoning—though such reasoning will never be as strong as that attained by doing a series of scientific experiments.

The three cases are not intended to be part of any cross-case logic. However, you may view them as attempted replications of the same theory—the importance and role of community partnerships. From such a standpoint, the more cases that can be arrayed in similar replicative fashion, the stronger the aggregate evidence in support of this broader theory.

SIMPLIFIED CASE EXAMPLE NO. 1: "TOWN MEETINGS GALVANIZE ACTION AGAINST DRUG DEALING"

In 1992, Bordertown, USA, recorded its highest homicide rate in history. Similarly, drug arrests and drug-related crimes were at high levels and had been steadily increasing. A new partnership—the Community Partnership Coalition (CPC)—charged its Anti-Drug Task Force (ADTF) to work with the community to identify the causes of crime and to identify solutions. The CPC, located in the Mayor's Office, organized a town meeting to hear citizens' opinions on crime. *This was the first attempt to bring together city residents to address these issues.*

Preexisting substance abuse problem

Partnership-initiated collaborative intervention

The meeting, which attracted more than 1,000 participants in November 1992, focused on several problems in the city, including drug dealing, abandoned houses, lack of community involvement, and various quality of life issues. *The CPC sponsored 15 follow-up neighborhood meetings among residents, police, public works officials, and others to identify specific problems and prioritize plans* to address these problems. In all but one neighborhood, residents cited drugs and drug dealing as the highest concern. These residents were asked to identify specific examples, such as the addresses of the abandoned houses and the exact street corners on which drug dealers were loitering.

Partnership planning

With the information provided by community residents, the CPC, through its ADTF, brought together town officials, the Bordertown Police Department, and the Department of Public Works. *This was the first time these parties had collaborated.* The result was the design of Operation Eliminate in May 1993, a two-pronged strategy that combined (1) specialized drug operations targeting both drug dealers and users that involved drug sweeps, sting operations, and buy-busts with (2) a streamlined process for demolishing abandoned buildings. The enforcement component was built upon existing narcotics enforcement practices; however, *the unique aspect of this new strategy was the involvement of the CPC, residents, and public works to identify targets.*

Distinctiveness of the collaboration

Collaborative activities

Operation Eliminate is funded in part by the town. The CPC also was able to secure corporate contributions to support the effort. The success of this effort has been contingent upon the active involvement of community members, starting with the CPC-sponsored neighborhood meetings, which continue to the present.

Table 5.1

Town Meetings Galvanize Action Against Drug Dealing

		Pre-1992	Post-1993	% Increase from 1992-1993
Law enforcement	Drug arrests	1,020	2,547[a]	149.7
	Marijuana seized	482 lb	2,452 lb[b]	408.6
	Cocaine seized	16 lb	349 lb[c]	2,029.8
Drug court	Jury trials	17	74	355.5
	Judge trials	2	0	0.0
	Guilty pleas	574	808	40.7

a 42.5% of drug arrests were logged by the Operation Eliminate unit.
b 11.0% of marijuana seizures were recorded by the Operation Eliminate unit.
c 4.0 % of the cocaine seizures were recorded by the Operation Eliminate unit.

A possible rival notion that Operation Eliminate resulted from a preexisting community policing initiative is not supported because the initial police division involved with Operation Eliminate was the narcotics division, not the community policing division.

Rejection of rival sources of support for intervention

As of April 1994, Operation Eliminate has resulted in *1,278 drug arrests and confiscations of 311 weapons. Overall, drug arrests in the city increased by 150% between 1992 and 1993, 43% of which are directly attributable to Operation Eliminate.* (See Table 5.1.) Statistics from the drug court, which is responsible for processing all drug offenders, indicate that *the quality of arrests also has improved, with guilty pleas for felony offenses increasing 41% after June 1993.* As a result of these arrests, *the police department has seized $678,962 in illegal narcotics. Also, since June 1993 when Operation Eliminate was implemented, the number of drug-related homicides has dropped by one third citywide.* In contrast to these trends, *other crime rates have remained the same or increased, providing no support for yet another rival explanation.*

Quantifiable outcomes and impacts

Outcome

Outcome

Rejection of major rival explanation for outcomes and impacts

The second prong of Operation Eliminate resulted in a reduction in the backlog of abandoned houses scheduled to be demolished, from 336 in 1993 to none in 1994. The time required to process building demolitions also decreased from 8 to 6 months, and the costs have dropped from an average of $2,000 in 1992 to $1,155 per building in 1993. Another positive indication of community involvement is the increase in the number of offenses reported to the police and to public works. Reported drug offenses increased 36%, and calls for service increased an average of 6% in high-crime areas in the 6 months immediately following the implementation of Operation Eliminate. *The evaluation team explored but found little support for rival explanations, including changes in the amount of drugs entering the city and the ongoing implementation of other police enforcement programs.*

Additional outcomes and impacts

Rejection of additional rival explanation

SIMPLIFIED CASE EXAMPLE NO. 2: "INTERAGENCY COLLABORATION TO REDUCE BWI INCIDENTS"

Until 1990, boating-while-intoxicated (BWI) incidents in the waters surrounding Seaside, USA, had been rising steadily. No apparent actions had been taken to address the problem. For instance, the U.S. Coast Guard, by mandate, focuses on water safety—not enforcement. The waterway enforcement agencies (Coast Guard, Harbor Patrol, and State Environmental Police) had been following an "enforcement by demand" policy, with little attention to BWI incidents and

Preexisting substance abuse problem

hardly any arrests. There were no BWI-specific patrols, blockades, or checkpoints by any of the three waterway enforcement agencies, nor were there any other related prevention actions.

A new partnership, the Seaside Prevention Network (SPN), was formed in January 1991. In initiating action, the SPN project director contacted the Coast Guard to identify ways of collaborating. Water safety (including substance abuse–related issues) was viewed as a point of common interest. Soon after, the SPN formed the Water Safety Coalition, in February 1991. The Coalition chose to focus its efforts on collaboration, community awareness, and training for boaters. These activities began almost immediately, with the SPN supporting community awareness campaigns and staff support for the water safety coalition.

Partnership-initiated collaborative intervention

Earlier, *the first federal regulation prohibiting the operation of a vessel while intoxicated had gone into effect in 1988. In 1992, an amendment established behavioral standards for determining intoxication.* The Water Safety Coalition's goal was to use this law to raise awareness and carry out preventive activities; no changes were ever attempted in enforcement practices.

Supportive contextual event

The Water Safety Coalition brought the three participating agencies together for the first time in their histories. When large recreational events were planned, the agencies would now coordinate their patrol efforts. *As another example, in 1993 the State Environmental Police and the Coast Guard developed an interagency agreement*

Absence of prior collaborative history

Distinctiveness of the collaboration

describing the role of each in concurrent jurisdictions.

The *community awareness activities* led to the placing of 300 BWl posters on marine gas pumps throughout the Seaside waters. The Coalition also mailed BWl information and safety tips to all mooring permit holders in Seaside and continues to do so on an annual basis. Related activities included bumper stickers, PSAs, newspaper articles, and education films for cable television.

Partnership activities

The Coast Guard Auxiliary, also a member of the Coalition, taught boating skills to junior operators by *coordinating junior operators' classes for state certification.* Thus far, 62 youths have received training to qualify for junior operator's licenses from the state. Throughout these activities, the SPN continued to provide funding, leadership, and staff support, which continues to this day. *The individual agencies also provided support, but no other sponsors were involved.*

Additional partnership activities

Rejection of rival sources of support for intervention

By 1993, a total of 14 BWI incidents (boardings resulting in arrests, accidents, or deaths) were reported by the Coast Guard, the Harbor Patrol, and the State Environmental Police, compared to a total of 35 reported incidents in 1990. (See Table 5.2.) Normalizing these incidents by the total boat traffic (monitored by a local bridge authority) also shows this downward trend, from .16% in 1990 to .05% in 1993.

Quantifiable outcomes

Table 5.2
Changes in Number of BWI Incidents

Law Enforcement Agency	1990	1991	1992	1993
USCG	30	19	10	8
Local	3	5	1	5
State	2	0	0	1
Total BWI incidents	35	24	11	14
BWI incidents as percentage of total boat traffic	.16%	.10%	.06%	.05%

SIMPLIFIED CASE EXAMPLE NO. 3: "DESIGNATED DRIVER PROGRAM, DELIVERED THROUGH VENDORS"

Summertown, along with surrounding vacation communities, experiences sharp seasonal increases in alcohol-related automobile injuries and deaths. Arrests for operating under the influence (OUI) exceeded the state average and caused concern among residents who wanted to maintain the tourist industry while providing for the safety of local citizens and visitors.

Preexisting substance abuse problem

The Summertown Partnership to Reduce Substance Abuse was formed in 1991. The issue of alcohol abuse was a primary concern, and efforts began immediately to find an effective remedy that would not undermine the tourist industry. A designated driver campaign had been planned and was in the early stages of implementation in surrounding communities. *The partnership adopted and expanded the campaign, developing the Safe Driver Program.*

Partnership formation

Partnership-initiated collaborative intervention

The partnership drafted *two drinking/driving policy initiatives* that—after testimony before local lawmakers and provision of safe-driver training and literature for the alcohol vendors and servers—were adopted by the town and the sheriff's department. The first policy was an ordinance requiring applicants for one-day alcohol sales to include a plan to prevent drinking and driving away from the event. The second policy strongly endorsed participation in the partnership's safe driver program, and the sheriff's department implemented the policy by informing all alcoholic beverage vendors and serving establishments.

Partnership activities

From the outset, change in OUI arrests was considered the criterion outcome measure. Further, although effective initiatives might be expected to lead to an initial rise in such arrests, eventually they must decline in order for an initiative to be deemed successful. Thus data have to be available for an extended period of time.

In Summertown, multiyear baseline data for the period prior to introduction of the program were compared to multiyear data for the period following implementation. The data showed that *compared to a rapid rise during the baseline period, OUI arrests began to decline slightly between 1990 and 1994.* (See Table 5.3.)

Quantifiable outcomes

Implementation of the Safe Driver Program was widespread, primarily because the partnership enjoys active support from the local law enforcement office and also from businesses that serve alcoholic beverages. *Because of the collaborative effort, an intervention was designed that enhanced the law*

Attribution to collaboration

Table 5.3
Outcomes From Designated Driver Program

	OUI Arrests June-August (1988-1994)	
	Year	Number of Arrests
Prior to program		
	1988	52
	1989	69
	1990	88
After program inception		
	1991	72
	1992	76
	1993	65
	1994	62

enforcement effort to reduce drunk driving without damaging business interests. Moreover, the OUI data—necessary for verifying the program impact—were accessible to the partnership because of the collaboration of the local law enforcement department, which is a partnership member. *This collaborative relationship did not exist prior to the formation of the partnership.*

Absence of rival collaborative history

The state launched a campaign against drunk driving during the period that the Safe Driver Program was being implemented. *However, other vacation communities reported an increase, rather than a decrease, in the number of arrests during the same period.*

Discussion of major rival explanation for outcome

6

Transforming a Business Firm Through Strategic Planning

Research on business firms has frequently assumed the form of case studies. The present case study demonstrates how explanatory case studies about such firms may be designed and conducted. The firm was a family-owned machine shop and components manufacturer. It had been pressured by its major customer to improve its production system or risk losing business. Implementation of cellular manufacturing solved the firm's initial production problems and resulted in a 300% capacity increase and a rise in employee skill levels and problem-solving capabilities.

However, in addition to the improved manufacturing processes, the firm's management team developed a shared, common direction about what to do with the company's extra capacity. The team undertook a strategic planning process that set the course for achieving long-range company goals and objectives in marketing, information systems, manufacturing, and human resources. The case study then documents the changes undertaken by the firm, showing how the combined effect of the changes went far beyond mere manufacturing improvement, effectively transforming the whole firm and its original organizational culture. Besides describing these processes, the case study explains how they led to the firm's successful growth in sales and profits.

Methodologically, the case study presents evidence from multiple sources (see Box 10). In many instances, the reported course of events represents a triangulation of the data from these multiple sources (see Box 11).

AUTHOR'S NOTE: This chapter is based on one of seven case studies appearing in *Transformed Firms Case Studies*, published by the National Institute of Standards and Technology (NIST), U.S. Department of Commerce, Gaithersburg, Maryland, April 1999. Robert K. Yin designed and directed the entire project, although each individual case study was conducted by a different person. The present case study was conducted by Jan Youtie. Prior to its appearance in the NIST document, the case study contained numerous additional footnotes and citations to specific sources of interview and documentary evidence. The version in this chapter has been condensed and edited.

BOX 10

Multiple Sources of Evidence

This case study of a transformed firm illustrates the use of multiple sources of evidence. Using such multiple sources strengthens case studies. In principle, evidence can come from at least six sources: documentation, archival records (e.g., computerized records of clients in a service delivery system), interviews, direct observations, participant observation, and physical artifacts (e.g., the actual condition of actual houses in a housing study). When findings, interpretations, and conclusions are based on such multiple sources, the case study data will be less prone to the quirks deriving from any single source, such as an inaccurate interviewee or a biased document.

(For more information, see Yin, 2003, Chapter 4, section on "Three Principles of Data Collection: Principle 1.")

BOX 11

Triangulation

Every, research investigator knows the original derivation of the concept of *triangulation*: A point in geometric space may be established by specifying the intersection of three vectors (not two or one, and four would be redundant). This concept has been borrowed for dealing with social science evidence: The most robust fact may be considered to have been established if three sources all coincide.

Consider the difficulty of establishing the occurrence of an event. You would be more confident in saying that the event had occurred if your study showed that information from interviews, documents, and archival records all pointed in the same direction. Most of the events reported in the present case reflect such a condition. This type of triangulation is the most desired pattern for dealing with case study data, and you should always seek to attain it. An important clue when doing your fieldwork is to ask the same question of different sources of evidence. If all sources point to the same answer, you will have successfully triangulated your data.

(For more information, see Yin, 2003, Chapter 4, section on "Three Principles of Data Collection: Principle 1.")

COMPANY PROFILE AND
CONDITIONS LEADING TO CHANGE

Rheaco, Inc., is a family-owned, privately held machine shop and components manufacturer. Located in the heart of the Dallas–Fort Worth
Metroplex in Grand Prairie, Texas, Rheaco provides full-service machining
and metal fabricating, primarily for defense customers. About 90% of its
business is in the defense industry.

Defense Industry Consolidation, Leadership Change,
and Rising Production Volumes Spur Changes

Rheaco's internal and external business environment experienced major
changes in the early 1990s. Rheaco's founder and president turned the
company over to his son, Rhea E. Wallace, Jr., in 1992. The same year and
following the Gulf War, Rheaco's major customer, Lockheed Martin,
began aggressively consolidating its supply chain, reducing the number of
its vendors from roughly 1,600 to 400 over a 2-year period.

Having survived this round of cuts, Rheaco had new opportunities to
supply parts to Lockheed Martin. Rheaco received orders for several
thousand additional parts, but the new orders choked Rheaco's production
system, which emphasized long production runs, long setup times, manufacturing to inventory, and the shipping of parts regardless of their quality.
In an earlier interview, Wallace had stated, "The company worked 7 days
a week for a year, with no letup."[1] Wallace had trouble locating orders
and did not have enough file cabinets for all the paperwork. Work in
process was so extensive that walking through the facility was difficult.
Occasionally, Rheaco's quality rating dipped below Lockheed Martin's
supplier specifications. Wallace's initial solution (to buy shelves and file
cabinets) added to the clutter. He even formed a team of 25 expeditors to
meet each morning, to determine the jobs needed to be completed by the
end of the day.

Change Process Begins With Solving Production System Problems

Wallace said, "It wasn't fun to come to work." He recognized the need
for change but did not have a specific plan. Instead, he took steps to solve
his immediate problem, which ultimately led to broad-based changes.
Wallace turned to third-party resources for problem-solving assistance and
for validating the ideas he had read about. Lockheed Martin provided some

help—seminars and hotlines—but it did not have an assistance program in the manufacturing process area.

In early 1992, Wallace and his management team attended a breakfast workshop series sponsored by the Automation and Robotics Research Institute (ARRI). Cosponsored by the Texas Manufacturing Assistance Center (TMAC), an affiliate of the Manufacturing Extension Partnership, the workshop series stressed creating a vision, changing company culture and dealing with people issues, and then adopting process and technology improvements. The series ended with a call for volunteers for in-company assessments to be conducted by TMAC or its affiliates.

Wallace volunteered his company for such an assessment. A specialist from the Small Business Development Center for Enterprise Excellence, a TMAC affiliate, conducted the assessment in late 1992. As part of the assessment, the specialist helped Wallace set up a process improvement team. The team first decided to work on paperwork issues and the ability to locate order information. The team, however, found that the paperwork problems were symptomatic of deeper production-floor problems.

In mid-1993, Wallace toured another small manufacturer, InterTurbine, which had experienced similar problems. InterTurbine had solved its production problems with cellular manufacturing, so Wallace concluded that cellular manufacturing was what his operation needed. Cellular manufacturing emphasizes small production runs, groupings of diverse equipment and machines, and manufacturing functions performed in close proximity to workers. These attributes represented a significant change from Rheaco's production system. Wallace decided to begin by implementing a three-person prototype cell in the metal extrusions area in the summer of 1993. That cell was successful, achieving a 200% improvement in throughput by its second week of operation.[2]

Because of this success and spurred by requests from other Rheaco workers to become involved in cells, Wallace implemented cellular manufacturing throughout the facility in late 1993 and early 1994. Rheaco's workers took 2 months to design the new facility layout. The 2 months of preparation allowed Rheaco employees to implement the new cells speedily, with minimal financial losses and downtime. Employees tore down the old workplaces overnight and implemented the new cells within a week. They created five manufacturing cells, one assembly team, and two plating teams, supported by five functional teams responsible for scheduling, quality, human resources, maintenance, and supplies.[3]

The August and September 1993 rollout also involved training managers and production-level workers in team processes and problem solving, so the cells could assume responsibility for each part. This level of responsibility required further training to enable team members to operate several types of machines and to manage different processes. Wallace set a goal of two qualified operators for each piece of equipment in each cell and promoted on-the-job cross-training to meet this "two-deep" goal. Designed to be self-directed, the teams eliminated the need for a foreman and moved the company toward a flat organizational structure.

Within the first year after converting to cellular manufacturing, Rheaco saw significant process improvements. Cellular manufacturing reduced work in process by 65%, material transport by 35%, and lead time by 87%. First-run yields improved 77%. Cycle times for videoconferencing card products declined from 120 days to 3 days, and production capacity increased by 300% without additional equipment or personnel. These improvements highlighted the need for less inventory, freeing 5,000 square feet of additional space.

Productivity improvements also reduced the need for workers, so 36 workers were terminated in 1993. Some employees, unable to handle the changes, decided to leave on their own. Shop-floor workers themselves made the remaining staffing decisions, based on factors such as perfor-mance, skills, and ability to be a team player.

STRATEGIC PLAN TRANSFORMS THE BUSINESS

Manufacturing processes had improved, but Rheaco's management team had no shared vision of what to do with the company's extra capacity. In the past, the company's founder had made all decisions about where to allo-cate company resources. Wallace's management style, as evidenced by the manufacturing cells and self-directed work teams, has been more participa-tory. Among the management team, members held diverse ideas about where to take the company and where its resources should be invested. The sales manager suggested that investments be made in new equipment, based on his discussions with customers about upcoming opportunities. Wallace's experience with cellular manufacturing identified the need for major expenditures on workforce training and quality certification. "Management was going in many different directions because we disagreed and lacked focus."[4]

Once Wallace had to spend less time solving daily production problems, he turned his attention to the development of a strategic plan. In the spring of 1996, he asked a TMAC manufacturing specialist to facilitate the strategic planning process for the company. The planning process involved developing a statement of purpose, assessing external strengths and weaknesses (including a customer profile), assessing of internal strengths and weaknesses, establishing strategic goals, identifying obstacles to realizing the goals, and developing actions for overcoming the obstacles. Members of the management team, representing human resources, finance, operations, customer service, and quality control, met weekly to produce the document.

The primary benefit of the strategic planning process was not just the planning document. Management team members reported that communications had improved. Team members achieved consensus on issues of company direction and allocation of company resources. "We were all on the same page," Wallace said. The customer service manager said that the planning process "brought everything to light."

The team decided to move from the company's traditional production-driven strategy to one oriented to customer needs. Analysis of costs and revenues by customer and by product identified which customer needs resulted in the most profitable business for Rheaco. To obtain this business, the planning team identified desirable strategic attributes: performing quick turnaround; developing advanced capabilities, such as five-axis machine technology for complicated surface parts; providing whole sub-assemblies; and offering full-service in-house capabilities in areas such as machine shop, painting, and plating. These attributes distinguished Rheaco from other machine shops. The impact of the strategic plan on other aspects of Rheaco's business is described below and summarized in Table 6.1.

Marketing Changes Target Valued Customers

In the marketing area, defense industry cutbacks and lack of long-term relationships with key customers made the company believe it had to "respond rapidly to the constant, unanticipated changing needs" of its customers.[5] Rheaco's move to cellular manufacturing made it more agile so that the account managers could "quote anything if the quantity was large enough." This approach produced large numbers of buyers to deal with and quotes to develop. Managing these multiple diverse relationships was difficult and time-consuming. Account managers had less time to prepare quotes and understand customer needs. Wallace, who served as account manager for most smaller accounts, endeavored to treat these 60 to 70 customers equally in terms of account management and delivery dates promised. This effort diverted his time from broader leadership efforts and impeded service to larger accounts.

Table 6.1

Rheaco's Systems Before and After Improved Strategic Alignment

Area	Before Strategic Planning	After Strategic Planning	Results
Management	• Lack of consensus about allocating company resources	• Single direction toward customer-oriented manufacturing	• President focuses on longer-range issues • Improved communication among management team • Involvement in community activities, such as apprenticeship program sponsorship
Marketing	• Difficulty prioritizing 54-70 customer jobs • Quoting inaccuracies	• Focus on a few key customers to become preferred supplier • Customer diversification initiatives	• Improved quotes • Sole-source provider for a number of parts • More sales at higher margins
Manufacturing	• Cellular manufacturing improved efficiency and capacity, and freed up space	• New business opportunities guided plant layout and investment decisions—e.g., investment in new penetrant inspection room • Pursuit of D1-9000 certification • Purified plating discharge • Achieved OSHA exemption	• Manufacturing capabilities match company strategy and market demand • Environmental, health, and safety measures support community commitment value in strategic plan
Information Systems	• MRP system did not integrate with accounting system	• New MRP system integrated manufacturing and accounting systems	• Material orders on time or ahead of schedule • On-time delivery of parts and

(Continued)

Table 6.1
(Continued)

Area	Before Strategic Planning	After Strategic Planning	Results
			components to customers improves, consistent with quick-turnaround customer satisfaction goal in strategic plan • Ordering material already in stock eliminated • Weekly assessment of financial status available
	• Weekly cash flow status not available • Materials were purchased late • Sometimes already-stocked items were purchased		
Human Resources	• Investment in machinery and equipment favored over employee training • Cellular manufacturing emphasized flat organization, self-directed teams	• Invested in people—e.g., hired penetrant specialist and retrained welders in penetrant inspection—as well as equipment to implement its new penetrant cell • Departed from flat cellular organizational structure by hiring general manager • Participated in developing community-wide apprenticeship program	• Human resources supports manufacturing, market demand, and company strategy • New general manager relieves president of ongoing shop-floor management • President focuses on strategic issues • Apprenticeship program supports community commitment value in strategic plan

SOURCE: COSMOS Corporation.

The strategic plan showed that Rheaco had a small number of profitable key customers. Rheaco's customer services unit changed its practices to focus on these customers. The customer services manager now has time to produce more accurate quotes and can obtain in-depth understanding of the customers' current and future needs. For example, Lockheed Martin has shared information with its Rheaco account manager about the amount of business it expects to subcontract in certain product areas. Rheaco has become a sole-source provider to Lockheed Martin for a number of parts and is selling a greater number of products at higher margins. Monthly revenues from major customers tripled in late 1998 from $20,000 to $60,000. Becoming a preferred provider has reduced the uncertainty in Rheaco's sales revenues. Focusing on major customers also enables Wallace to devote less time to minor customer account management and more time to broader strategic issues.

Rheaco's strategic plan called for diversifying into commercial aerospace markets. Rheaco's planning team determined that the commercial aerospace industry was a good fit with its existing defense business. The plan calls for understanding the needed qualifications for doing business with aerospace firms. Rheaco is currently targeting its marketing and quality efforts at this new customer segment.

Manufacturing Systems Support Customer Needs

Rheaco's traditional approach to manufacturing systems was to invest in machines that could run large volumes of parts. With the introduction of cellular manufacturing, the company arranged equipment and workers to improve efficiency and free up space, but what the company should do with its additional capacity and space was not clear.

The strategic plan played an important role in guiding the company to use using its newfound manufacturing capacity. Significant new business opportunities now guide plant layout and investment decisions. For example, improved understanding of a major customer's plating needs led Wallace to purchase new plating equipment. Another example involves Rheaco's new "penetrant inspection" cell built in 1998 to conduct nondestructive testing for cracks, leak paths, and other structural defects. An account manager had learned that Lockheed Martin needed quick turnaround service in this area. Wallace decided to use the excess space from the cellular manufacturing implementation to build a penetrant inspection room. These two examples illustrate Rheaco's ability to rearrange manufacturing cells based on where the company can make money.

To meet the other goal of the strategic plan—diversifying into commercial aerospace markets—Rheaco's quality manager is pursuing

Boeing D1-9000 certification. Wallace said that before the process changes and strategic plan, "I didn't even have enough confidence to get certified." Rheaco met Lockheed Martin's quality requirements and those of other major defense customers. Rheaco had won various quality awards, such as the 1993 Loral Vought Systems Subcontractor of the Year Award (even as the company was converting to cellular manufacturing) and the 1994 Small Business Administration's Administrator's Award for Excellence. However, the company had never undergone standards certification. The plan identified quality certification as a major goal and the lack of Boeing D1-9000 certification as an obstacle to customer diversification. Rheaco's quality manager is currently leading the quality team in assessing manuals, training, and conducting audits, and working with TMAC quality specialists to achieve Boeing D1-9000 certification.

Pursuing Boeing D1-9000 certification and basing facilities investment decisions on customer needs demonstrate the alignment between the production system and Rheaco's strategic plan. Although the cellular manufacturing implementation had solved Rheaco's production capacity concerns, manufacturing capabilities matched company strategy and market demands only after Rheaco completed its certification.

Rheaco Invests in Human Resources

In the human resources area, the strategic plan directed hiring decisions. Despite the human resource changes associated with Rheaco's cellular manufacturing initiative, the planning process revealed that the company's investment emphasis on machinery and equipment over human resources hindered the accomplishment of the strategic goals. Rheaco's managers decided to allocate resources based on skills needed to bring in specific business. For example, Rheaco wanted to deliver penetrant inspection services, but it lacked in-house expertise. Therefore, Rheaco hired a specialist to help design a penetrant inspection cell for the shop floor and provide training. To implement its new penetrant cell, Rheaco invested in people as well as equipment.

In addition, Rheaco hired a general manager in 1998 to deal with the day-to-day responsibilities of the manufacturing operation. Although this addition conflicted with Wallace's desire for a flat organization, the management team reached consensus in the planning process that the shop floor needed a general manager. The new general manager quickly relieved Wallace of ongoing shop-floor management responsibilities.[6]

Information Systems Changes Improve Customer Service

In the information systems area, the strategic planning process revealed problems with Rheaco's old manufacturing resource planning (MRP) system. This system was not integrated with other systems and was not regularly used. Consequently, the purchasing department made errors in ordering materials. For example, sometimes orders were not placed until after the final delivery date, and at other times the purchasing department ordered materials already in stock. The strategic plan called for an integrated information system.[7] In 1998, Wallace purchased a new MRP system that combined manufacturing and accounting systems. The new system significantly improved the purchasing function. The purchasing manager now orders and receives materials on time or ahead of schedule, which has improved the on-time delivery of parts and components to customers. These improvements have enhanced Rheaco's ability to be a quick turnaround shop and to meet its customer satisfaction goal of 100% on-time delivery. Wallace also uses the system to assess the company's financial situation weekly rather than waiting until the end of the month.

Rheaco Enhances Its Community Involvement

One of the strategic plan's major goals was to "be actively involved in our community."[8] Community involvement, according to the management team, included environmental, health, and safety compliance, as well as participation in community programs. In 1998, Rheaco participated in the Safety and Health Achievement Recognition Program and received a Certificate of Recognition award from the U.S. Department of Labor's Occupational Safety and Health Administration (OSHA), exempting the company from programmed OSHA inspections, a first for Rheaco. Wallace joined with 15 other small manufacturers and Bell Helicopter in sponsoring an apprenticeship program in the Fort Worth Independent School District. Rheaco hired three graduates from the first two graduating classes.[9]

Sales and Wages Increase Along With Supplier
Consolidation in Tight Labor Market

Total sales increased 56%, from $3.5 million in 1992 to $5.4 million in 1997. Revenue per employee improved by 90% over the same period, and value added per employee (revenue minus wages, per employee) increased 175%, from $16,317 in 1992 to $44,930 in 1997 (see Figure 6.1). Rheaco's sales increase arguably may have resulted from changes made by Lockheed

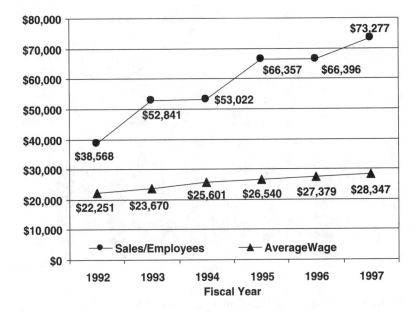

Figure 6.1.   Rheaco's Sales and Wages per Employee, 1992-1997

Martin, whose supply chain consolidation provided opportunities to Rheaco and other preferred suppliers, including higher value-added components and subassemblies business. Nevertheless, Lockheed Martin's supplier management practices cannot fully explain Rheaco's sales increases. Without its extensive changes, Rheaco could have been eliminated as a supplier in later rounds of consolidation. Lockheed Martin's additional specialized needs might have been missed without Rheaco's strategic goals in the account management area. Clearly, Rheaco's new customer orientation in marketing and other areas resulted in substantial sales increases.

Rheaco's consistent sales increases allowed it to increase its employee investments. The number of employees has risen from a low of 67 to 85, nearing pre-layoff levels. Nevertheless, payroll expenses as a share of sales revenue dropped from 58% to less than 40% from 1992 to 1997, reflecting Rheaco's increased productivity (see Figure 6.2). Wage increases also occurred, in part, because of a tight labor market: The unemployment rate in the Fort Worth–Arlington area dropped to 3.1% in October 1998 (compared with 4.4 % nationwide).[10]

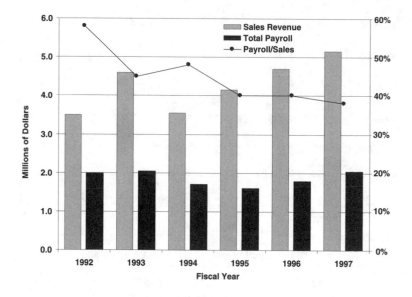

Figure 6.2.   Rheaco's Business Performance, 1992-1997

Strategic Planning Guides Multiple Interrelated
Changes to Make Rheaco a Transformed Firm

This case study demonstrates that Rheaco is a transformed firm. First, Rheaco made multiple changes throughout all major company systems. Rheaco had been a soundly operated firm prior to these changes and had survived Lockheed Martin's massive supplier consolidation. Rheaco also had won quality awards prior to or simultaneously with converting to cellular manufacturing—and well before it initiated strategic planning. However, even recognizing these accomplishments, Rheaco had experienced fundamental production problems in the early 1990s that threatened its customer relationships. Cellular manufacturing initially addressed these problems, but ultimately it was the planning process that prompted multiple and interrelated changes—for example, improving the alignment in the company's systems in support of market needs and business strategies.

The totality of the transformation produced Rheaco's significant gains in financial performance. Lockheed Martin's supplier consolidation gave Rheaco opportunities, but Rheaco could not have exploited these opportunities, much less have profitably expanded them, without its broad-based and interrelated changes. By aligning the company's systems, Rheaco moved from a capacity-driven job shop to a customer-driven, high-precision supplier. Consequently, the total effect of the changes on firm performance became greater than the sum of the effects of individual changes.

CHRONOLOGY

1991-1992: Felt pressures of defense downsizing, which threatened business with largest customers.

Early 1992: Rhea E. Wallace, Jr., took over as company president. Company had 94 workers. Wallace and other Rheaco managers attended Breakfast Workshop Series cosponsored by the Texas Manufacturing Assistance Center (TMAC).

Late 1992: Small Business Development Center for Enterprise Excellence (SBDC) representative conducted an in-company assessment.

February-March 1993: SBDC representative helped Rheaco set up process improvement team. Team decided to focus on paperwork processing problem.

June-July 1993: Managers visited InterTurbine.

August-September 1993: Implemented prototype manufacturing cell in metal extrusions area. SBDC representative provided training for 25 managers and shop-floor workers. Won Loral Vought Systems Subcontractor of the Year Award.

November 1993-February 1994: Implemented cells throughout production floor and set up team structure.

May 1994: Won U.S. Small Business Administration's Administrator's Award for Excellence.

End of 1994: Workforce dropped to 67 workers.

1995: Work in process declined by 65%, material transport reduced by 35%, lead time dropped by 87%, first-run yields improved 77%, cycle times for videoconferencing cards reduced from 120 days to 3 days, and production capacity increased by 300%.

November 1995: Won Blue Chip Enterprise Initiative Award.

Spring 1996-1997: Management engaged in strategic planning process, facilitated by TMAC representative; established "two-deep program"; developed plan for effective quoting system; partnered with Bell Helicopter and 15 other companies to offer machinist apprenticeship program and hired three program graduates.

First quarter of 1998: Participated in the Safety and Health Achievement Recognition Program.

April 1998: Qualified for exemption from programmed OSHA inspections.

Second half of 1998: Hired penetrant inspection specialist and built penetrant inspection cell. Began pursuit of D1-9000 certification. Hired new general manager. Bought new MRP system. Had 85 workers.

December 1998: Welders received penetrant inspection training.

NOTES

1. Yudken, Joel S., & Blackerby, Phillip. (1998, September). "Rheaco, Inc.," in *MEP Successes: Workforce Development Case Studies,* p. 63. Gaithersburg, MD: National Institute of Standards and Technology.

2. Underdown, Ryan, & Mills, John. (1995, June 15). "Agility: A Small Defense Manufacturer Can Do It Too!" *Manufacturing News,* p. 9.

3. Company documents: "Old Rheaco Floor Plan" and "World Class Rheaco."

4. Rheaco Strategic Plan, "Internal Weaknesses," 1996.

5. Yudken & Blackerby, p. 72.

6. Organization Chart, Rheaco, Inc.

7. Rheaco Strategic Plan, "Strategic Goals," 1996.

8. Rheaco Strategic Plan, "Values," 1996.

9. Yudken & Blackerby, p. 71.

10. U.S. Bureau of Labor Statistics, December 1998.

7

Sheriff's Combined
Auto Theft Task Force

In the public sector, innovative practices have served as another familiar topic of case study inquiry, often taking the form of case study evaluations (see Box 12). The common evaluation question has been the extent to which (a) external funding (e.g., an award from the federal government) led to (b) an innovative practice that in turn produced (c) desirable and documentable outcomes. Explanatory case studies are one way of tracking the presumed sequence of events.

The present case study focuses on the creation of a 14-county auto theft task force that provided cross-jurisdictional authority to the deputies in all of the counties. One claim is that federal funds helped to create this unprecedented, multicounty law enforcement collaboration. A second claim is that the collaboration's series of activities reduced the auto thefts in the area. The chapter shows how a relatively short case study can address such claims.

Critical to the line of evidence is tracking the chronological sequence of events. For instance, regarding the first claim, state-level funds were available and being used earlier than the federal funds. However, the chronology shows how the state funds were not used to support collaborative efforts or needed equipment purchases prior to the availability and use of the federal funds.

AUTHOR'S NOTE: This is a revised version of 1 of 18 case studies that were part of an evaluation report titled *National Evaluation of the Local Law Enforcement Block Grant Program: Final Report for Phase I*, COSMOS Corporation, March 2001, whose main author was Robert K. Yin. (The complete evaluation was based not only on the set of 18 case studies but also on the results from two large-scale surveys of law enforcement agencies.) Different staff persons at COSMOS conducted and composed the original case studies, which all followed a similar protocol and methodology. Revisions have been made to illustrate more clearly the organization of an explanatory case study.

BOX 12

U.S. General Accounting Office (GAO) Guidelines
for Doing Case Study Evaluations

This chapter presents 1 of 18 case studies selected because each represented an innovative practice, not a representative group of practices. The goal was to explain how and why federal funds had produced innovative practices. In this sense, the case studies all might be considered evaluative case studies.

The U.S. General Accounting Office (GAO) has been among the more frequent users of case studies as an evaluation tool. To help its own evaluators, GAO published a comprehensive methodological report titled *Case Study Evaluations* (1987/1991). The report's usefulness and detailed operational advice make it an invaluable document for all others in the field (for example, studies evaluating interventions in such areas as justice, housing, welfare, environment, education, and foreign aid.)

Throughout, the GAO report emphasizes quality control and rigor and therefore freely adapts many of the procedures and concepts from earlier editions (Yin, 1984/1989/1994) of the companion text to this book (Yin, 2003), such as the use of multiple sources of evidence, the establishment of a chain of evidence, and the reliance on pattern matching and explanation building as two major analytic strategies.

(For more information, see Yin, 2003, Chapter 1, section on "Variations in Case Studies.")

THE PRACTICE AND ITS FUNDING

Four major highways intersect the central Texas region, providing thoroughfares for offenders engaged in interstate and international auto theft. For example, automobiles stolen in Travis County (which includes the city of Austin) are transferred to surrounding rural counties, where their vehicle identification numbers (VINs) are altered to facilitate resale; the vehicles are "chopped" (dismantled for sale of parts, which are often more valuable in the illegal market than the total vehicle); and the parts are consolidated for transshipment. Rural areas (especially those with little auto theft activity and limited law enforcement coverage) provide excellent locations for "chop shops" that support organized auto theft from neighboring counties and cities. The counties cover a broad expanse—averaging more than 700 square miles and with population densities reaching as low as fewer than 10 persons per square mile.

Earlier, Single-Jurisdiction Efforts

Beginning in 1991, the Texas Auto Theft Prevention Authority (ATPA), supported by a $1.00 premium per insured automobile per year assessed to all Texas vehicle insurance companies, had funded several projects in a statewide attempt to reduce vehicle-related criminal activity.[1]

ATPA made state funding available to single jurisdictions (cities or counties), even though auto theft crime networks operated across jurisdictional boundaries and transported stolen vehicles from populous areas into rural locations, increasing the likelihood of avoiding detection. Furthermore, funds were to be used for personnel salaries but not for equipment. The allocation of funds was formula driven, based on the UCR (Uniform Crime Reporting) auto theft reports by each location. Theft of farm or industrial equipment was not considered, nor was the location of recovered vehicles. To a great extent, ATPA funding supported prevention programs and targeted criminals who could be caught in the act; however, it did not provide for multijurisdictional approaches that would identify chop jobs and consolidation areas in isolated, nonpopulous regions favored by organized crime.

Multijurisdictional Efforts

Recognizing the need for a multicounty cooperative effort to reduce auto-related criminal activity in central Texas, the Travis County Sheriff's Office took the initiative in 1997 and expanded its auto theft unit to create the Sheriff's Combined Automobile Theft-Prevention Task Force (SCATT). The regional task force united the 14 law enforcement agencies in the counties of Bastrop, Bell, Blanco, Burnet, Caldwell, Colorado, Comal, Fayette, Hays, Lee, Llano, Milam, Travis, and Williamson. The initiative was facilitated by the availability of federal funds administered under the Local Law Enforcement Block Grant (LLEBG) program.

LLEBG funding, with its flexibility in allowing the local determination of expenditures, provided for the purchase of equipment needed to strengthen communications between Travis and surrounding counties, prompting the formation of the SCATT Force. Once these working relationships had been established, Travis County applied for and was awarded increased funding by ATPA to provide salaries for additional officers who were to be assigned to the participating counties. In 1996, the Travis County auto theft unit received $162,000. In 1997, SCATT's potential was recognized by an increase to $350,000. It is now considered the most effective task force in the state and will receive $497,000 from ATPA in 1999.

SCATT has been one of the few multicounty law enforcement task forces in the state. Because of the independent natures of Texas's counties and sheriffs, some have even conjectured that it might be the first such collaboration in history. Before its formation, car-theft-related law enforcement was reactive and essentially driven by the need to satisfy the Uniform Crime Reporting system. Available data showed that the vast majority of automobile thefts occurred in the high-population areas of Travis County (population 710,000), with some occurrences in Bell (223,000) and Williamson (224,000). The remaining 11 counties have a combined population of less than 400,000 and lacked both the incidence rates to generate citizen concern and the resources to respond effectively, even if auto theft were a problem.

A Complementary Initiative

Help End Auto Theft (HEAT), a statewide vehicle registration program, was implemented in 1993 to assist law enforcement officers in identifying stolen vehicles throughout Travis and surrounding counties. Participating vehicle owners sign an agreement stating that their vehicles may be stopped between the hours of 1:00 a.m. and 5:00 a.m. or when crossing the border into Mexico. An identifying decal in the rear window enables Texas law enforcement officers to observe and stop vehicles to verify ownership. HEAT is a primary prevention program for SCATT, using officers to support a public education and awareness campaign throughout the 14-county region. This effort recognizes that 94% of all recovered vehicles are related to amateur, joyrider outings, whereas the remaining 6% constitute the work of professional thieves who feed organized criminal networks—the primary interest of SCATT.

IMPLEMENTATION OF THE PRACTICE

In 1996, a newly-elected Travis County Sheriff recognized that although auto theft was increasing in the county, the number of recovered vehicles was not matching the increase. Pressure on Travis County chop shops had driven such operations to barns and isolated buildings outside the county and beyond the reach of the Travis County Sheriff's auto theft unit.

Despite the lack of any history of cross-jurisdictional cooperation, the sheriff emphasized the need for improved law enforcement communication across county boundaries because such boundaries were not observed by the region's organized-crime-supported auto theft network. However, the budgets of the surrounding county sheriffs' offices were unable to support a compatible radio system or to patch into the Travis County system. The issuance of cell phones to deputies was the most reasonable alternative. Even this outlay was nevertheless impossible to make because the surrounding counties, most with populations under 30,000, had no equipment budgets, and the Travis County budget authority was not likely to approve using its sheriff's budget to fund another county's operation, no matter how small.

The LLEBG moneys awarded to the Travis County Sheriff's Office provided the funding and flexibility at an especially opportune time. Having spent the previous 6 months developing interest in a multicounty task force, "talking the talk," the Travis County Sheriff "walked the walk" by diverting LLEBG funds to the 13 surrounding counties, to purchase the equipment needed to coordinate services.

SCATT began in September 1997. The 14 sheriffs selected the Travis County Sheriff to be the standing chair of a Board of Governors that included a representative from every county, and which was provided "the power to conduct investigations, make arrests without a warrant, execute search warrants, and make other reasonable and necessary law enforcement actions for the purpose of and in pursuit of achieving Task Force objectives *outside the jurisdiction from which the officer is assigned* and within the territory of a specific Task Force operation." To support SCATT's structure, all 14 sheriffs formally signed an Interlocal Assistance Agreement,[2] and SCATT provided the smaller counties with the equipment and manpower needed to identify vehicle-related criminal activity (i.e., chop shops). In the past, the less populous counties had insufficient resources to conduct surveillance or investigate potential stolen vehicle trafficking. Many could not provide basic patrol during the late-night and early-morning hours and were not inclined to devote scarce resources to a crime that, because of its rarity in rural counties, was perceived as a Travis County or Austin problem. As SCATT became operational, rural counties recognized their role and responsibility in combating a larger organized crime network. They also began to focus on thefts of farm vehicles and construction equipment that often went unreported and were usually not missed by owners for days or weeks after the theft.

This comprehensive network continues to encourage communication between the county sheriffs and provides prevention, detection, and interdiction related to vehicular theft. Each county is covered by additional officers placed in adjoining jurisdictions as needed by the Travis County Sheriff's Office. Because the additional sheriff's deputies are recruited from and reside in counties to which they are stationed, they not only bring local knowledge but also create a trusting and cooperative atmosphere across county lines.

The Task Force's initial focus on stolen vehicles paved the way for cooperation on other law enforcement matters (e.g., revenues from vehicle thefts were found to support the purchase of illegal drugs for distribution) and also led to additional collaboration with the Drug Enforcement Agency (DEA); Bureau of Alcohol, Tobacco, and Firearms (ATF); and other state agencies. Furthermore, Travis County began to utilize its crime lab to support investigations by SCATT sheriffs for crimes other than car theft.

SCATT holds formal monthly meetings to prioritize activities and plan coordinated operations. As needed, other law enforcement entities (such as the U.S. Attorney's office, ATF, DEA, Texas Rangers, and Customs) are participants at the meetings. SCATT officers, as part of their routine investigative duties, also are authorized to interface with their counterparts in these agencies between meetings.

The original cooperative effort would not have been possible without the LLEBG funding. Now, SCATT is institutionalized in all 14 counties with local support and will no longer require LLEBG funding.

OUTCOMES TO DATE

The SCATT Force is a fully operational unit providing services in interdiction, field training, salvage yard inspections,[3] covert interdiction, overt interdiction, and public awareness.

From September 1997 to April 1999, SCATT trained 665 officers, many from counties outside the SCATT area, in 31 classes; uncovered 18 chop shops; recovered vehicles valued at over $7.5 million; and recovered $550,000 in property. Typical of the effect of Task Force collaboration was an operation described in the *Austin American-Statesman* in June 1999:

> Authorities (officers from the Travis County Combined Auto Theft Task Force, working with a U.S. Drug Enforcement Agency task force from the Waco area) have arrested at least two people suspected of being part of a ring of thieves who have stolen $400,000 in trailers, loaders, and a backhoe from construction sites in Travis and Williamson counties during the past 6 months. . . . The suspects in the thefts are also suspected of trafficking in methamphetamines. ("Theft ring targeting building work sites," *Austin American-Statesman,* June 17, 1999)

The following figures summarize SCATT's progress during fiscal year 1998-1999, also demonstrating how prior goals continue to be exceeded:

- *Training*: 23 classes taught, with 383 officers participating. Stated goal: Members of the Task Force will conduct a total of 18 training classes for the law enforcement agencies within the 14-county area, to educate the officers on how to locate, detect, and recover stolen vehicles.
- *Public awareness:* 38 demonstrations performed. Stated goal: Agents of the Task Force and its participating agencies will conduct a total of 24 public awareness services to the public within the 14-county area by promoting auto theft prevention and the HEAT program through Task Force agents, crime prevention officers, community policing officers, and the use of several forms of media.
- *Salvage inspections:* 117 inspections performed. Stated goal: Agents will conduct a total of 80 inspections of the following auto-related businesses:

A. Unlicensed salvage yards

B. Licensed salvage yards

C. Auto body and repair shops

D. Wrecker/Storage yards

E. Garage and mechanic shops

F. Auto auctions

G. Inspections for the public

H. Used car lots

I. Auto crushers

- *Checkpoints:* 45 performed. Stated goal: Agents of the Task Force will conduct 12 auto theft checkpoints; due to the laws and legalities of surrounding checkpoints, the following operations will be utilized to conduct these checkpoints:

A. Working with license and weight officers at weigh stations

B. Working "Operation Gate"

C. Making stationary parking lot checks

D. Checking boat ramps

E. Marking checkpoints by using signs stating "Checkpoint Ahead"

F. Highway interdiction

- *Chop shops:* Nine uncovered. Stated goal: Agents of the Task Force will search out and locate five chop shops within the 14-county area.

- *Intelligence information:* Nine submitted. Stated goal: The Task Force will distribute auto theft intelligence information to all agencies within the 14-county region via the *Travis County Intelligence Bulletin.*

- *Decrease in auto theft:* During the first year of the grant, field agents have had tremendous success identifying stolen vehicles. Auto-related arrests made by unit investigators increased from 6 in the first quarter to 18 in the second. The Task Force has had 4 seizures and inspected 69 salvage yards in the first 2 quarters. In the first 2 quarters of the LLEBG grant, the Task Force recovered 232 stolen vehicles. Those vehicles represented a value of approximately $2.4 million. By mid-1999, the year-to-date auto thefts had declined by 25% (from 368 per 100,000 residents the previous year to 276 per 100,000 residents). Stated goal: Decrease the overall auto thefts in the 14-county area.

CHRONOLOGY

1991: Establishment of the Texas Automobile Theft Prevention Authority (ATPA) by the 72nd Texas Legislature, to create a statewide effort to reduce vehicle theft. (Statewide, 164,000 auto thefts were reported in 1991, with an average loss per vehicle of over $5,000.)

1992: Travis County receives first funds from ATPA to support auto theft unit.

1993: ATPA funds the *Watch Your Car HEAT* program. Window decals authorize officers to apprehend a vehicle between the hours of 1:00 a.m. and 5:00 a.m.

1996: The new Travis County Sheriff explores creation of a multicounty regional task force to combat auto theft.

1997: Travis County's LLEBG funds are used to purchase cell phones and other equipment. The SCATT Force is established. Fourteen county sheriffs are represented on the Board of Governors, headed by the Travis County Sheriff. LLEBG funds support two additional deputies assigned to SCATT.

1997: Interlocal Assistance Agreements provides cross-jurisdictional authority to SCATT Deputies.

1997: ATPA increases Travis County's award from $160,000 to $350,000, for expanded multicounty activities.

1998: ATPA increases SCATT award to $400,000.

1999: ATPA awards SCATT $497,000, which supports eight deputies and a public information specialist.

2000: LLEBG funds no longer required for SCATT.

REFERENCES

[The original case study cited 10 documents as references and six persons who had been interviewed during the site visit.]

NOTES

1. ATPA funds are distributed through a grant process, primarily to eligible counties and cities. Categories for projects eligible for funding include activities such as enforcement/apprehension, prosecution/adjudication, public education, prevention of sale of stolen auto parts, and reduction of stolen vehicles moved across the Mexico border.

2. The Interlocal Assistance Agreement, Regional Auto Theft Enforcement Task Force, was entered into pursuant to Chapter 791 of the Texas Government Code, concerning interlocal cooperation contracts, and Chapter 362 of the Texas Local Government Code.

3. The Sheriffs' Combined Auto Theft Task Force conducts extensive salvage yard inspections throughout the 14 counties. Each inspection ensures that persons involved in the business of salvaging and repairing vehicles conduct their business in accordance with the laws of the state of Texas.

PART IV

Cross-Case Analyses

8

Technical Assistance for HIV/AIDS Community Planning

This cross-case analysis covers the findings from eight explanatory case studies. Each case study evaluated the provision of technical assistance (TA) to a community planning group (CPG) by covering a single TA episode as the unit of analysis. (A single episode could nevertheless have extended over multiple occasions.) The TA was provided by one or a combination of organizations that the Centers for Disease Control and Prevention (CDC) had designated as part of a network known as the TA Network. The types of TA assumed the form of workshops, consultations, hands-on assistance, and the provision of materials, in any mixture. The CPG was to use the TA to develop annual community plans to allocate funds for HIV/AIDS prevention.

The cross-case analysis starts by clarifying the theoretical framework underlying the data collection for the eight cases, especially clarifying the nature of the relevant outcomes related to the TA episodes being studied. The cross-case analysis then presents the data from the eight case studies, using a replication logic (see Box 13)—the overall evaluation question having to deal with explaining the performance of the TA Network as a whole, not the results from any single TA episode. Also distinctive about the cross-case analysis is the explicit identification of rival explanations (events other than the TA) that might have been alternative reasons for the observed outcomes. The cross-case analysis concludes by reviewing the strength of evidence for eight hypotheses that were defined at the outset of the evaluation, before any of the individual case studies had been conducted.

AUTHOR'S NOTE: The original cross-case analysis appears in the *Final Report for the Evaluation of the CDC-Supported Technical Assistance Network for Community Planning,* Vol. I, COSMOS Corporation, July 1999, by Robert K. Yin. The complete evaluation was based on two separate studies, and the eight individual case studies and the present cross-case analysis comprised one of these studies. The original text has been lightly edited for readability.

BOX 13

Replication, Not Sampling Logic, for Multiple-Case Studies

The selection of the eight case studies in the present chapter followed a replication, not sampling, logic. This means that all eight cases were chosen because they were claimed to have had positive outcomes beforehand. The case studies and the ensuing evaluation then predicted that similar processes would be found to account for these outcomes (direct replications). If such replications are indeed found for several cases, you can have more confidence in the overall results. The development of consistent findings, over multiple cases or even multiple studies, can then be considered a more robust finding.

Sampling logics are entirely different. They assume that an investigation is mainly interested in representing a larger universe. The selected cases are therefore chosen according to preidentified representation criteria. These logics do not work well with multiple-case studies; they distort the benefits of using the case study method in the first place. In fact, if sampling logic is important to an inquiry, survey methods are more likely to satisfy an investigation's needs than is the case study method.

(For more information, see Yin, 2003, Chapter 2, section on "What Are the Potential Multiple-Case Designs?")

INTRODUCTION: A FRAMEWORK FOR ASSESSING THE EFFECTIVENESS OF TECHNICAL ASSISTANCE (TA)

Defining the Outcomes of Interest

The desired and meaningful outcomes of any HIV prevention effort might normally be expected to be assessed in relation to *reductions in the incidence of HIV/AIDS*. To this extent, the work of a TA network should simply be evaluated in terms of this outcome.

However, such a straightforward expectation is not reasonable (and may not be possible), because the TA Network's assistance is not aimed directly at reducing HIV/AIDS incidence. In fact, the assistance occurs, logically, at a much earlier step in a much elongated process. The array of steps in the full process might be considered as follows:

1. CDC mandates that each CPG implement a *community planning process*. The TA Network is mainly formed to assist CPGs in carrying out this planning process.

2. One outcome of the planning process is a *comprehensive prevention plan*, reviewed annually by CDC. The plan indicates how prevention resources are to be allocated among a variety of HIV prevention services, based on the CPG's analysis of its community's existing needs and services.

3. The state or local health department associated with the CPG presumably allocates *prevention resources* according to the plan, and the resources are used to support HIV prevention services.

4. *HIV prevention services* are implemented. In order to be effective, the services must (a) follow an appropriate design, properly targeting a priority population; (b) be implemented well; and (c) overcome other conditions in order to reduce HIV/AIDS incidence.

5. Only if all the preceding steps have occurred properly will the desired ultimate outcome—a *reduction in HIV/AIDS incidence*—occur.

Figure 8.1 depicts these steps in the form of a logic model (see Box 14). The sequence of steps suggests that the TA Network's assistance mainly occurs at the first step, whereas the ultimate desired outcome of prevention occurs at the fifth step. Such a relationship means that the TA Network's work is *distal* with regard to the ultimately desired HIV prevention outcome. In other words, any reduction or change in HIV/AIDS incidence in a community is likely to be affected only indirectly by the work of the TA Network.[1] The outcome is more likely to be affected by many other conditions, including the manner in which the intervening steps are followed. Reduction in HIV/AIDS incidence is therefore not a good benchmark for judging the TA Network's effectiveness.

Given this framework, the TA Network was assumed to be more fairly assessed in relation to the success of the community planning process as an outcome. Such a process was assumed to consist of three functions that became the subject of outcome evaluation:

1. Better-functioning CPGs

2. Improved planning processes

3. Production of better comprehensive community plans

Selecting the Case Studies

To evaluate the TA Network, eight case studies were selected. Each case study covered a TA episode as the unit of analysis (see Box 15) in which

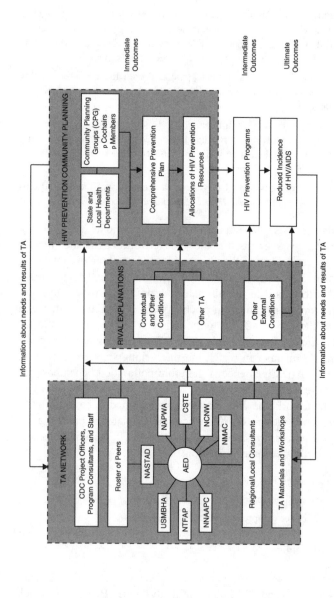

Figure 8.1. Relationship Between TA Network and Desired Outcomes

AED = Academy for Educational Development; CDC = Centers for Disease Control and Prevention; CSTE = Council of State and Territorial Epidemiologists; NAPWA = National Association of People With AIDS; NASTAD = National Alliance of State and Territorial AIDS Directors; NCNW = National Council of Negro Women; NMAC = National Minority AIDS Council; NNAAPC = National Native American AIDS Prevention Center; NTFAP = National Task Force on AIDS Prevention; USMBHA = U.S.-Mexico Border Health Association

---

BOX 14

Logic Models

The multiple steps taken to reduce HIV/AIDS may be considered a repeated series of activities and outcomes. Such a hypothesized sequence of activities and outcomes comprise a process that can be organized and depicted as a logic model. Case study data can then be analyzed to test the plausibility of the hypothesized sequence, to determine whether the actual sequence of events emulates the hypothesized one.

Articulating the logic model can even be considered an end in itself. For instance, in evaluating public programs or organizational changes such as those in the current chapter, sometimes the planned change is discovered to be illogically related to its desired outcomes, on intuitive grounds alone, without needing any actual empirical evidence (Wholey, 1979). The establishment of a compelling logic model is therefore essential in two respects. First, it can guide the implementation of any planned change. Second, evaluation teams should establish that a logical model is in place—that is, one that makes common sense—before proceeding with data collection and the remainder of an evaluation.

(For more information, see Yin, 2003, Chapter 5, section on "Logic Models.")

---

the TA Network was known beforehand to have produced desirable outcomes. In other words, the cases were exemplary and not representative, chosen from about 25 nominations. Although all were exemplary, the cases were intended to reflect a variety of TA modes and topics.[2]

The inquiry also sought to examine *how* the TA Network had produced any desirable outcomes and thus to *explain* the work of the TA Network. In conducting the inquiry, the evaluation team therefore also developed a series of hypotheses regarding the conditions that were believed to be important in producing the desired outcomes.

Collecting the Data

For each case study, the evaluation team conducted a site visit to the CPG that had received the TA. Discussions also were held with the CDC staff person who was the project officer at the time the TA was provided. The site visits called for interviews with the key participants in the TA, as well as the collection of relevant documents and archival materials. As a

---

BOX 15

The Unit of Analysis: A Critical Concept in Doing Case Studies

The eight case studies in this chapter are about organizations providing technical assistance to health agencies in eight states. However, the unit of analysis for the cases is neither the organizations nor the agencies. Rather, each case focuses on a specific technical assistance engagement, which is the actual unit of analysis.

No issue is more important than defining the unit of analysis. "What is my case?" is the question most frequently posed by those doing case studies. Without a tentative answer, you will not know how to limit the boundaries of your study. Because case studies permit you to collect data from many perspectives—and for time periods of undetermined duration—you must clearly define the unit of analysis at the outset of your study.

The unit of analysis has another critical significance in doing case studies. The findings of the case study will pertain to specific theoretical propositions about the defined unit of analysis. These propositions will later be the means for generalizing the findings of the case study—to similar cases focusing on the same unit of analysis. Thus the entire design of a case study as well as its potential theoretical significance is heavily dominated by the way the unit of analysis is defined.

(For more information, see Yin, 2003, Chapter 2, section on "Components of Research Designs.")

---

result, the case studies attempted to track the actual course of events, going beyond those field studies that largely focus on open-ended interviews and hence are limited to reports of participants' perceptions.

Upon completing the site visits, the materials for each case study were compiled into a formal database (a collection of narrative and numeric evidence organized according to the topics in a case study protocol). The databases also included individual logic models, showing the claimed flow of events in each case, starting with the conditions that existed prior to the TA episode to the outcomes of the TA. These logic models represent the confirmed events of the cases and therefore their presumed causal flow. Drafts of the databases were shared with the participants at the original sites, for review and comment, and corrections and comments were incorporated into the final versions. The remainder of this chapter discusses the outcomes and varieties of TA that were studied, an examination of rivals, and the findings for each hypothesis.

DOCUMENTED OUTCOMES, VARIETIES
OF TA STUDIED, AND POSSIBLE RIVAL
EXPLANATIONS FOR THE OUTCOMES

Outcomes Associated With the TA From the TA Network

Table 8.1 summarizes the outcomes from the eight case studies. Originally, the summaries were to emphasize the community planning process outcomes. However, an unexpected finding was that in six of the eight cases, the outcomes of the TA appear to have gone beyond the planning process and influenced the next phase of the process—HIV/AIDS prevention service delivery.

Table 8.1 shows that in every one of the cases, the TA did affect the community planning process. For instance, nearly every case demonstrated the TA's influence on better-functioning CPGs. The specific outcomes were substantiated by both interviews and documentary evidence in the eight case studies.

Also as shown in Table 8.1 is the influence that went beyond the planning process, which included such steps as the design of a subsequent request for proposals (RFP) used by the health department or CPG to solicit service delivery proposals from local agencies and organizations (Mississippi, North Carolina), outreach to minority and ethnic programs (Idaho, Montana, Utah), and changes made by community-based organizations (CBOs) to improve or revamp their prevention programs (Montana, Nebraska).

The fact that the successes include not only the community planning process but also the HIV/AIDS prevention service delivery process was not anticipated in the original evaluation design and therefore may be considered a positive, unanticipated outcome from the evaluation of the TA Network. Again, because of the way the eight cases were selected and screened, the frequency of similar experiences in other TA episodes is unknown.

Varieties of TA Associated With the Outcomes

TA delivery involves the substantive topics of the TA and also the modes for communicating the TA, including on-site visits by TA providers, the provision of materials, and telephone consultation. The experiences of the eight case studies provide examples of all these modes of delivery. Of the cases, seven involved TA on-site visits. Although not the most prominent

Table 8.1

Outcomes Associated With TA by the TA Network

| | Effect on Community Planning Process | | Effect on Service Delivery | |
State	Better-Functioning CPGs	Improved Planning	Better Comprehensive Plan	Allocation of HIV Prevention Resources	Implementation of HIV Prevention Services
Florida (Statewide)	CPG members have enhanced appreciation of epidemiologic profile as driver of further planning steps.	Completed epidemiologic profile for the entire state.	—	—	—
Florida (Miami-Dade)	Groups with history of hostile relationships reach consensus on the consolidation process.	New (county) ordinance enacted, creating consolidated planning organization; new (city) ordinance still being sought.	—	—	—
Idaho	Formation of statewide CPG and seven regional CPGs; statewide CPG develops bylaws.	Priority populations are identified using epidemiologic data.	CDC judges application, previously out of compliance, to be in compliance in 1996 and 1997.	Program funding is established for a number of priority populations.	—

(Continued)

Table 8.1
(Continued)

State	Effect on Community Planning Process			Effect on Service Delivery	
	Better-Functioning CPGs	Improved Planning	Better Comprehensive Plan	Allocation of HIV Prevention Resources	Implementation of HIV Prevention Services
Mississippi	Two African American women, attendees at forum, join the CPG.	Health department designs additional forums targeting other at-risk groups.	—	CPG issues RFP shortly after forum and makes multiple awards, including cultural pride program with HIV education as main focus.	—
Montana	Improved relationship between statewide CPG and Native American Advisory Committee (NAAC); NAAC more involved in community planning process.	Statewide planning group selects research-based HIV prevention interventions; bases priority setting on data in the epidemiologic profile.	CDC finds 1996 plan in compliance with community planning guidelines.	Seven Native American tribes receive contracts for the first time to provide HIV prevention services; 14 county health departments and a CBO also receive contracts.	Prevention services are research-based.
Nebraska	Participants gain better understanding of community planning	—	—	—	Some CBOs improve or revamp programs around effective interventions.

(Continued)

Table 8.1
(Continued)

State	Effect on Community Planning Process		Effect on Service Delivery		
	Better-Functioning CPGs	Improved Planning	Better Comprehensive Plan	Allocation of HIV Prevention Resources	Implementation of HIV Prevention Services
	and of role as CPG members; statewide and six regional CPGs operate more efficiently; members share ideas more comfortably.				
North Carolina	—	—	CDC accepts revised plan in September 1998 (original priority-setting had failed to weed anything out).	CPG issues new RFP to solicit proposals reflecting new priorities.	—
Utah	CPG develops better screening process for membership; African American participation has increased.	Conference participants help CPG identify ways of reaching ethnic and minority populations.	—	Two CBOs serving ethnic communities apply to health department for funding after conference; CDC provides additional funding for CBOs.	—

SOURCE: COSMOS Corporation (1999).

delivery mode, on-site TA may have a greater impact than other modes of communication because of its intensity. The possibility therefore exists that the outcomes would not have occurred had only off-site or other modes of communication been used to deliver the TA.

Table 8.2 itemizes the characteristics of the TA for each of the eight case studies. The first column in the table shows that not only did seven of the eight involve on-site TA, but in most cases, the TA occurred over an extended period of time, involved multiple on-site events, or both. These cases therefore represent instances of long-term TA, the implication being that the observed outcomes might not have occurred if the TA had only been short term.[3]

The second column of Table 8.2 shows the diversity of TA topics covered by the eight cases, in part a result of a case selection process that deliberately sought such diversity. The main objective in so doing was to see whether desirable outcomes tend to be limited to one or a small set of TA topics, and the observed diversity suggests no such limitation.

The third and fourth columns in Table 8.2 show the recipients of the TA and the apparent role of the various partners in the TA Network in arranging and supporting the TA episode. Neither column contains any surprises: The recipients most often include a public health department and the CPGs, and the TA Network's involvement ranges from situations in which a single partner made the entire arrangement and provided the entire support (Florida—statewide, Miami-Dade, Montana, and Nebraska) to those where multiple partners were involved (Idaho, Mississippi, North Carolina, and Utah).

As an additional note, the case studies had difficulty defining the TA recipients because most TA providers believe that they are delivering TA to an organizational unit (e.g., the CPG), whereas the specific knowledge imparted by the TA provider appears mainly to be imparted to a small group of individuals. No data were collected, however, to confirm which individuals actually benefited from a TA episode, or even to test whether the CPG as an organization had been affected.

Rival Explanations for the Observed Outcomes

The preceding analysis suggests that an array of desirable outcomes has been produced by the TA provided by the TA Network. To test this claim further, the case studies deliberately sought data regarding rival explanations (see Box 16) for the same outcomes. Four types of rivals were considered across the eight cases, and Table 8.3 lists these and the evidence collected about them.

Table 8.2

Varieties of Technical Assistance Associated With Eight Case Studies

	Characteristics of the Technical Assistance (TA)			
State	Mode	Topic	Recipient	Role of the TA Network
Florida (Statewide)	Two months' on-site TA, with follow-up visit; off-site TA for following year, including additional on-site TA at two training workshops	Development of epidemiologic profile for whole state and for two local examples	Mainly the Division of Sexually Transmitted Diseases/HIV/Tuberculosis in health department	CSTE fully arranges and supports this TA, involving one of its staff. The engagement would not necessarily have been recorded or tracked as part of AED's coordinating role.
Florida (Miami-Dade)	On-site TA, with multiple TA consultants participating in several meetings and public forums during a single event	Development of partnership model for streamlining HIV prevention planning across four federal programs	Steering committee, local health department, and other local (not state) participants	TA is provided by one external consultant and two external peers, all arranged and supported by AED.
Idaho	Extensive on-site TA at conference and off-site TA following conference, combined with TA provided by a regional (non-TA Network) provider	Community planning process, development of epidemiologic profile, and development of comprehensive plan	The health department, as well as participants who would become part of the statewide or seven regional CPGs	AED, CSTE, and NASTAD staff and consultants all participate, each organization covering its own costs but with AED coordinating the on-site TA and continuing to arrange needed follow-up TA.

(Continued)

Table 8.2
(Continued)

State	Characteristics of the Technical Assistance (TA)			Role of the TA Network
	Mode	*Topic*	*Recipient*	
Mississippi	On-site TA involving presentations and facilitation at a forum	PIR and outreach to African American women	Health department, as well as a CBO selected to target services to African American women	AED arranges and supports TA by NAPWA and NCNW staff persons, selected in conjunction with request by health department.
Montana	On-site TA involving three separate events, each several months apart	Priority-setting, assessment, and behavioral science	Mainly CPG and health department	AED arranges and supports TA by its staff and by consultants.
Nebraska	On-site TA involving multiple statewide and regional events occurring over a 9-month period	PIR, community planning, harm reduction, evaluation, AIDS 101 and social marketing	Mainly CPG and health department	AED arranges and supports TA by its staff and by consultants.
North Carolina	Off-site TA involving materials and information provided over a period of several months	Priority-setting and epidemiologic profile	Two local TA consultants (immediate recipients); CPG (indirect recipient)	NASTAD and CSTE provide information at the request of two local TA consultants. The local consultants, in turn, do on-site work with the CPG and health department (paid by the health department).
Utah	Multiple on-site TA at different annual events	PIR and outreach to ethnic minorities	Health department and the CPG	USMBHA staff person presents and facilitates at annual meeting, arranged directly with health department. AED arranges and supports outside consultant and own staff at later annual meeting.

SOURCE: COSMOS Corporation (1999).

121

BOX 16

Rival Explanations

No concept is more helpful in conducting research than the concept of *rival explanations.* Yet, existing texts rarely point to the importance of this concept, much less giving guidance on how to articulate or investigate such rivals.

The most common rival explanation has been the null hypothesis. A null hypothesis is simply that the observed effect or outcome occurred by chance alone and not because of any hypothesized intervention. However, in doing case studies, possibly the more important rivals are those that point to other plausible conditions or forces that might have produced the observed effect or outcome. If you have identified rival explanations in this sense, you can collect data to test all competing explanations and compare the results through a pattern-matching process. The better and more numerous the rivals that can be investigated in this manner, the stronger your case study will be—whether the bulk of the evidence supports the originally hypothesized intervention or not.

(For more information, see Yin, 2003, Chapter 5, section on "Three General Strategies.")

The data show some support for three of four rivals (Rivals 1, 3, and 4 in Table 8.3). For instance, Rival 3 shows that complementary conditions, such as the provision of TA by those not in the TA Network (e.g., local TA providers, or consultants to or staff of the health department), existed in three cases (Idaho, North Carolina, and Utah). However, no support was found for Rival 2, as only one instance of TA by another federal program was encountered; this TA occurred later and appears to have been irrelevant to the observed outcomes.

In general, none of the rivals was supported to the extent of completely undoing the claimed connection between the TA Network's work and the observed outcomes. Rather, the examination of rival explanations supports the basic conclusion that the work of the TA Network appears to have played a prominent role in producing the observed outcomes, in spite of the coexistence of other relevant conditions.

Table 8.3

Rival Explanations for Outcomes Observed in Eight Case Studies

---

Rival 1: CPGs will achieve the same goals, just not as quickly and not necessarily to the same extent, without technical assistance (TA) from the TA Network.

- The TA accelerated efforts to complete the epidemiologic profile, even though the state was on its way to making similar changes on its own. However, the resultant TA product also was of outstanding quality and represented innovative ways of presenting and interpreting data. (Florida—statewide)

- Staff of the health department made a concerted effort to fund ethnic and minority groups, and (in conjunction with the TA) contributed to greater participation by and targeting of services to minority groups. (Utah)

Rival 2: The important TA was provided by other federal sources, not just the TA Network.

- Additional assistance was provided by another federal program. However, this assistance occurred later and did not affect the recommendations of the TA Network's assistance, nor did it instigate any move toward implementing the plan for streamlining prevention planning across four federal programs. (Miami-Dade)

Rival 3: The important TA was provided by local groups, consultants, or health department staff, not just the TA Network.

- At the same time that the TA Network was providing TA, the health department and CPG also had been engaging a regional TA group to assist with meeting facilitation, community organizing, and meeting planning. The regional TA group also interfaced with the TA Network and provided TA to the regional CPGs within the state. However, although the presence of the regional TA group contributed to the improvement of the state's community planning process, it is doubtful that the regional TA group could have provided the type and level of TA that came from the TA Network. (Idaho, Montana)

- The TA Network assisted two local TA providers; the providers themselves brought their own expertise, on complementary topics, that helped to produce the outcomes. (North Carolina)

- Efforts by the health department staff, not just the TA Network, contributed to greater participation of minority groups in community planning and greater targeting of services to minority populations. (Utah)

Rival 4: CPG membership is enhanced by conditions other than parity, inclusion, and representation (PIR) and the outreach facilitated by the TA Network.

- Four African American women joined the CPG; however, two did not join the group as a result of the forum assisted by the TA Network, as they did not even attend the forum. (Mississippi)

SOURCE: COSMOS Corporation (1999).

FINDINGS ON INDIVIDUAL HYPOTHESES REGARDING REASONS FOR SUCCESSFUL TA DELIVERY

Beyond the documentation of the observed outcomes and support for their claimed link to the work of the TA Network, the examination of specific hypotheses developed at the outset of the evaluation were intended to produce other lessons learned about the TA Network, aimed at strengthening the network. The main findings and implications to be drawn from each hypothesis are discussed next.

H_1: Joint Definition of TA Needs:

Successful TA will result when TA needs are jointly defined by the TA users and the TA providers (e.g., by the CPG and the TA providers in the network).

Findings. At least two steps need to be taken to define any TA assignment. The first is to determine the need for TA. Once such a determination has been made, the second is to produce a refined definition of the TA to be provided. When first stipulated, H_1 did not distinguish between these two steps. The eight case studies helped to clarify the steps as well as the role of TA users and TA providers in both of them.

With regard to the first step, nearly all organizations in the TA Network affirmed that the CPG or the CDC project officer had been the dominant definer of the initial need for TA. The TA providers are not usually involved in this process, so that there is little, if any, joint definition of the TA need.

In the second step, the specific TA providers do become involved in refining the understanding of needed TA. For instance, a TA provider will have repeated conference calls or other discussions on defining the specific TA events to be supplied (e.g., Nebraska, Idaho). However, situations may arise where the TA provider works with a CPG representative who is not fully knowledgeable of the TA needed by the CPG. As a result, the ensuing TA may not be as well defined or received as it could have been, as occurred in one of the eight case studies (North Carolina). For this second step, a critical question may therefore be the identity and knowledge of the CPG representatives who act as the TA user in defining the needed TA.

Possible Implications. The findings suggest that to strengthen the TA Network, more attention should be given to the identity of the specific person(s) in the CPG (and his or her professional expertise) who represents the CPG in defining the needed TA. To the extent that a CPG contains sub-groups with uneven technical skills, any TA provider who follows the advice of one or a small number of CPG representatives in defining the needed TA risks the possibility of defining TA that will not meet the CPG's initial needs.

An institutional remedy would be to have all CPGs appoint a TA sub-committee charged with covering both steps and then also evaluating the TA. This TA subcommittee would then be the main point of contact between any TA provider and the CPG. The subcommittee would be charged with engaging all the TA on behalf of the CPG, including local and regional providers engaged directly by the CPG and not through the TA Network. Such an oversight subcommittee would then be more likely to represent multiple views and also cumulate the benefits of the TA over time and across TA providers.

H$_2$: Externally Defined TA Objectives:

The community planning process is improved and plans are found to be more comprehensive when TA objectives are externally defined, as a result of a peer or CDC review of comprehensive plans or through CDC project consultants' monitoring activities.

Findings. TA episodes may be defined not only by TA users and TA providers but also as a result of CDC's external reviews, which occur annu-ally and cover the adequacy of a CPG's comprehensive plan as well as the health department's official application for the upcoming year of prevention (not just planning) funding. TA needs most often arise when the external review has judged a state's submission to be out of compliance (e.g., Idaho, Montana, Utah) or a specific component of the plan, such as priority setting, to be unsatisfactory (e.g., Montana, North Carolina).

When TA objectives are externally defined in this manner, subsequent comprehensive plans usually are found to be more compliant with CDC's requirements. The case studies also showed that the community planning process was improved and the plans were better targeted for prevention ini-tiatives. The first column of Table 8.4 lists the experiences in the eight cases, indicating that external reviews initially played a role in defining the TA needs for half of them (Florida—statewide, Idaho, North Carolina, and Utah).

Over the course of the first 4 years, nearly all the CPGs' comprehen-sive plans have come to meet CDC requirements, reflecting the five core

Table 8.4

TA Features Related to Three Specific Hypotheses Discussed in Text

State	H_2: Extent of External Definition of TA Objectives by CDC's External Reviews	H_3: Extent That TA Providers Are From Multiple TA Organizations	H_4: Extent That TA Episode Consists of Multiple TA Events
Florida (Statewide)	External review identified four limitations with State's epidemiologic profile	All TA is provided by staff from one TA organization, CSTE.	CSTE staff person provided TA over an extended period of time, covering 2 months on site and later followed by two other on-site visits, including training workshops (hence, multiple TA events).
Florida (Miami-Dade)	CDC's external reviews played no role.	All TA was provided by one TA organization, AED. The individual TA providers were a TA consultant and two peer representatives, all arranged and supported by AED.	There were several TA events (an open committee meeting, a public meeting, and a local summit). However, all events occurred within the same month.
Idaho	External review found project area out of compliance with community planning guidelines.	TA involved staff or consultants from three different national TA organizations (AED, CSTE, and NASTAD), as well as a regional TA organization.	Major TA event was a conference; however, continued TA was arranged by AED for the following 2 years.
Mississippi	CDC provided supplemental funds to health department to support outreach to minorities.	TA involved staff from two TA organizations, NCNW and NAPWA, both selected by the TA recipient.	TA consisted of a single TA event—a forum.

(Continued)

126

Table 8.4
(Continued)

State	H_2: Extent of External Definition of TA Objectives by CDC's External Reviews	H_3: Extent That TA Providers Are From Multiple TA Organizations	H_4: Extent That TA Episode Consists of Multiple TA Events
Montana	External review found state to be out of compliance with CDC's community planning guidance.	TA is provided by one TA organization and by state health department staff.	TA consisted of three events occurring over a year-long period.
Nebraska	CDC's external reviews played no role.	All TA was provided by one TA organization, AED. The individual TA providers were both AED staff and consultants.	TA was provided at multiple events over about a 6-month period (hence, multiple TA events).
North Carolina	CDC's external review rejected the state's plan for 1996-1999, taking issue especially with the priority-setting effort, which in CDC's view, "failed to weed anything out."	All TA was provided by two local TA providers. They worked together and received off-site TA from two national TA organizations (CSTE and NASTAD), and AED also kept record of the TA.	The two local TA providers delivered a series of TA events over a multimonth period; CPG pondered how to produce updated plan to cover next 3-year period.
Utah	CDC's external review found the project area to be out of compliance in 1996.	TA was delivered by staff from USMBHA as well as consultants and staff from AED.	TA was provided at multiple events over a period of about 12 months.

SOURCE: COSMOS Corporation (1999).

objectives (CDC, 1998). Furthermore, CDC has indicated a continuing desire to "raise the bar" by adding new issues to be addressed over and above the five core objectives (CDC, 1998). Over time, as CDC continues to expect more from the community planning process, the process is likely to improve and the plans to become increasingly comprehensive.

Possible Implications. Continuation of the direct link between the external reviews, the availability of TA, and compliance requirements is likely to lead to continued improvements in the planning process. Furthermore, CDC should emphasize giving early signals to the TA providers regarding emerging requirements. Such early signals are needed so that the TA providers have time to assemble the needed expertise, anticipate the likely calls for new TA, and prepare high-quality responses.

H₃: Collaboration of TA Providers:

When multiple individuals provide TA to a CPG, TA is more successful when the TA providers collaborate.

Findings. Collaboration among TA providers was defined as an occasion when persons representing two or more TA Network organizations provided joint TA. (The two persons might have been staff or consultants.) The overall frequency of such occasions is not clear, although the likelihood is that such TA is only a low proportion of all the TA. For instance, the tracking of all TA episodes by the Academy for Educational Development (AED) shows that most of the episodes involve AED staff or consultants. Among the eight case studies, the proportion of joint TA was much higher (see column 2 in Table 8.4, which shows four of the eight having involved collaborative TA—Idaho, Mississippi, Montana, and Utah), but the eight cases are not claimed to be representative of the entire universe of TA provided by the TA Network.

The TA providers reported that collaborative TA, especially when involving on-site TA, does not occur more often because of its high cost, as well as the increased difficulty of scheduling such events to suit the TA providers and maximizing local participation (AED). Thus one TA provider noted that such a collaboration would be likely only when a CPG was in need of TA on multiple topics (CSTE).[4] This type of situation appears in at least one of the eight case studies (Idaho), in which a broad variety of TA was provided to address the project area's multiple needs.

At the same time, all TA providers expressed satisfaction with those occasions when collaborative TA was provided, because the individual providers can see how their own special topics fit better with the other topics, and the CPG can derive benefit from the explicit cross-linkages that can be created (CSTE). Some of the TA organizations, however, have only rarely collaborated with others (e.g., NAPWA).

Possible Implications. The high cost of collaborative TA efforts means that every collaborative effort might displace several singular TA episodes (given the costs of arranging and scheduling, and not just delivering the TA). The results are nevertheless beneficial, especially if a CPG has a complex or broad array of needs.

As a result, one possibility is for organizations in the TA Network to budget, at the outset of any given year, a small and explicit number of collaborative TA episodes, apart from the singular TA episodes. The TA Network would then set priorities for using these resources devoted to collaborative TA, separate from the resources devoted to singular TA. Such division of resources might increase the control over and effective use of the limited TA resources.

The resources for joint TA should be used on those occasions when two or more different skills and issues are at stake—for example, PIR (parity, inclusion, and representation) and epidemiologic profiles, or competition among two different minority groups within the project area. Such situations would appear to make the best use of this more costly type of TA.

H_4: Series of TA Events:

Successful TA experiences involve a series of TA events that build on and support each other.

Findings. The notion of a series of TA events overlaps with the TA Network's definition of long-term TA. For instance, AED's TA briefing book for CPGs (AED, 1995, p. 7) defines short-term TA as limited phone consultation, one-time visits, and nonrecurring consultation with local, regional, or national TA providers. Long-term TA is defined as more than one site visit, or coordination among local, regional, or national providers over a period of time. Most of the TA providers did not distinguish between short- and long-term TA and could not provide information on the advantages of one over the other.

Column 3 of Table 8.4 shows the distribution among the eight case studies. Six of the eight cases involved multiple events, or long-term TA (Florida—statewide, Idaho, Montana, Nebraska, North Carolina, and Utah). Such long-term TA could include one or more on-site visits, spread apart and interspersed with phone TA (Florida—statewide). Some long-term TA extended over a period of a year or more (Idaho, Utah). Other long-term TA needs follow the annual cycles imposed by CDC, with a priority-setting plan, for instance, in need of being updated with the onset of the new planning cycle for the coming year(s) (North Carolina).

Possible Implications. The TA Network should continue to provide both single-event and series TA, not favoring one over the other. The TA Network might also consider routine follow-up assessments of the effectiveness of on-site TA, 1 to 2 months following an event, and holding a conference call with CPG representatives, the CDC project officer, and the TA providers to discuss follow-up or additional TA needs. AED currently follows this procedure, but the others in the TA Network do not. The objective would be to provide ongoing support to CPGs and to continually reinforce the importance of the community planning process and a responsive comprehensive plan. Follow-up TA could involve providers from the TA Network or from local TA providers.

H_5: Coordination With Other Federal Agencies:

Successful TA provided by the TA Network is coordinated with HIV prevention and community planning TA provided by other federal agencies.

Findings. Few instances of coordination of the community planning process for HIV/AIDS prevention with community planning and prevention programs of other federal agencies were uncovered by the case studies or mentioned by the providers in the TA Network. On the rare occasions that coordination did occur, it was related to coordinating CDC's community planning with the three prevention-planning mandates other than CDC—Ryan White I and II and HOPWA (Miami-Dade). The possible benefits from such coordination were considered sufficiently high in this particular case that a local ordinance was enacted to create a single planning body.

CPGs and TA providers believe that the federal agencies themselves need to collaborate first, before encouraging any coordination at the project area level (AED). The requirements of the various federal programs have not been especially coordinated to date, and the fear is that the CPGs will get stuck with an entirely new set of problems that could have been averted had the federal agencies first taken care of matters properly.

Possible Implications. Any intention or plan to have the TA Network emphasize greater coordination across federal programs needs to be

approached cautiously. Until it is evident that the requirements and procedures are more compatible, attempts at starting coordination at the local
level might be difficult.

H₆: Informing National TA Providers of TA Network Activities:

*The TA Network is more effective when national TA providers are
informed of the activities of the overall TA Network.*

Findings. TA assignments generally focus on a single specialty such as
needs assessment, epidemiologic profiles, PIR, or conflict resolution. Some
TA providers are not necessarily knowledgeable about the other specialties
in the process and especially about whether TA has previously been provided to a CPG with regard to the other specialties. For instance, there was
no formal procedure in place, reported by the TA providers, whereby part
of the preparation of a new TA episode would include retrieving information on any previous TA to either the same CPG or on the same topic (nor
was there any database that included all previous TA done by all the TA
organizations).

Over time, all members of the TA Network have become better informed
about specialties besides their own, with at least two positive effects. First,
diagnostic capabilities, and therefore the precision of referrals, have
increased (AED), potentially leading to better TA outcomes. Second, at
least one individual TA organization noted that when pursuing its own specialty, knowledge or awareness of other specialties was useful in linking
the TA to the other specialties. In this case, assistance on epidemiologic
profiles was considered more useful when the TA provider was aware of
the latest needs assessment and priority-setting practices being promoted,
so that the epidemiologic profile could be better connected to the needs
assessment and priority-setting procedures (CSTE).

Possible Implications. Thus far, the TA Network has relied mainly on
informal procedures to share information about its own activities and specialties, although more formal sharing has begun to occur. An example of a
more formal procedure is the monthly conference calls among the TA
providers that were started early but suspended for a while and then
resumed in early 1998, as well as recent face-to-face meetings that occur in
conjunction with other meetings. In this manner, the TA providers are using
conferences and annual meetings as the occasion for holding working sessions among themselves. These and other modes of sharing should continue
to be encouraged.

H₇: Reactive and Proactive TA:

Both reactive and proactive TA need to be available.

Findings. The TA providers have traditionally assumed a reactive posture, at least with regard to on-site TA, and make no claims to being proactive (AED, CSTE, USMBHA, and NAPWA). In other words, although the availability of TA has been made known through general channels (including distribution of pamphlets as well as communication through CDC project officers and other word-of-mouth techniques), the TA providers make no solicitations to specific CPGs regarding possible TA assignments. Whether specific local/regional TA providers have been proactive to any significant extent is unknown.

The most proactive TA possibly occurs when a CPG has been found to be out of compliance with CDC's guidelines by its external review. In some of those situations, the CDC project officer may alert the project area to the need for TA and, in this sense, serve as the active agent (e.g., Idaho, Utah). Thus, in this sense, proactive TA is available.

Possible Implications. Unless CDC establishes a further rationale for proactive TA, the availability of proactive TA is likely to be limited to compliance situations.

H₈: Long-Range TA Planning:

The planning process is more successful when CPGs engage in long-range TA planning in addition to serving other needs.

Findings. None of the case studies showed strong evidence of long-range planning for TA on the part of the CPGs. Some TA episodes, such as assistance in establishing a single planning body to deal with the possible coordination of four federal programs (Miami-Dade), involved issues that would have potential long-range implications. However, the TA itself was not long-range. Evidence of the need for long-range planning arose in at least one case (North Carolina), where CPG members were concerned over their ability to update upcoming prevention plans, having benefited from TA on earlier plans. However, no mechanism had been put into place to anticipate the specific TA needs that could arise.

Possible Implications. A standing TA subcommittee or task force as part of every CPG, previously discussed under *H₁* above, could serve as a coordinating body to increase consistency across TA episodes. This same subcommittee could define and plan for long-range TA, which might be to the benefit of many if not all CPGs.

NOTES

1. The TA Network is one of several TA providers on the community planning process. Local TA providers, for example, may also influence community planning. Distinguishing the impact of the TA Network on community planning, much less on the later steps (including HIV/AIDS prevention), is difficult.

2. A separate methodology section in the original report describes the entire process for nominating, screening, and selecting the eight cases.

3. The possibility exists that the nominating process was biased in favor of long-term TA. Short-term TA (involving only one on-site event) may not have been sufficiently memorable (or might have been viewed as being too common or producing effects that were too transient) to be worthy of nomination.

4. This and other organizational acronyms are decoded in Figure 8.1.

9

Proposal Processing by Public and Private Universities

Explanatory case studies can be helpful in the absence of a formal intervention. Explaining how universities develop their research proposals and at what cost were the main topics of a series of case studies of 20 individual universities (see Box 17). The results from each university were compiled in a series of formal databases submitted as appendices to the final report. The cross-case analysis was based on the information in these databases.

The participating universities deliberately represented a variety of research- to non-research-oriented universities, large and small, that were geographically distributed across the country. Data were collected either through site visits or through lengthy telephone interviews combined with additional documentation. Because the proposal development process at a university can involve several different academic departments and administrative offices, data were collected from a large variety of sources, usually involving contacts and interviews with over 15 individuals at a given university.

The research team also retrieved quantitative data estimating the level of the proposal costs from an archival source—the proportion of the universities' indirect costs reported annually to the federal government. The resulting cross-case analysis therefore not only illustrates the

AUTHOR'S NOTE: This chapter presents excerpts from an original cross-case analysis that was part of a report titled *The National Science Foundation's FastLane System Baseline Data Collection: Cross Case Report*, COSMOS Corporation, November 1996. The excerpted text has been lightly edited for readability, with leader dots indicating the omission of substantial positions of the original text. Robert K. Yin was the main author of the report.

The study collected data from 20 universities, of which 15 were collaborating with the National Science Foundation (NSF) in the development of the FastLane system—the first system created by a major federal research agency to enable grantees to submit their proposals and reports electronically. The purpose of the study was to document the conditions among these universities prior to the start of the electronic system. The baseline results could then be compared to the results from some future study, to be conducted any number of years later (to date, such a study has not been commissioned).

BOX 17

Importance of Multiple-Case Studies

All the case studies in this book, whether presented as single- or multiple-case studies, were originally part of a multiple-case study. If given the choice (and the resources), multiple-case designs may be preferred over single-case designs. In particular, if you can even do a two-case study, your chances of producing robust results will be better than using a single-case design. For instance, analytic conclusions independently arising from two cases, as with two experiments, will be more powerful than those coming from a single case (or single experiment) alone. You also can avoid a common criticism about single-case designs—that the choice of cases reflected some artifactual condition about the case—for example, special access to a key informant or special data—rather than any theoretically compelling argument.

(For more information, see Yin, 2003, Chapter 2, section on "Single- or Multiple-Case Designs?")

---

use of qualitative and quantitative data but also led to a surprising finding—that those universities producing larger numbers of proposals also had higher costs per proposal, a pattern contrary to the normal expectation based on an economies-of-scale logic. The results were subjected to statistical analysis, showing how such analysis is possible even with a modest number of cases. These findings were compared to a qualitative analysis that had placed the universities in several categories—another example of the use of a replication logic in a cross-case analysis—to suggest why the unexpected relationship had been found.

The study was not an evaluation. However, from an evaluation perspective, a legitimate shortcoming is that the study did not cover the important outcomes of interest—not simply the proposals produced but rather the number and proportion of winning proposals and their total dollar amount. In this sense, from an evaluation perspective, the entire cross-case analysis might be considered an example of a process evaluation (see Box 18).

INTRODUCTION TO THE STUDY

This cross-case analysis is based on data collected from 20 universities about their 1994-1995 proposal processes. The study was to collect baseline

---

BOX 18

Process Evaluations

Producing research proposals may be considered a *process*, which should then yield a sequence of desired outcomes: winning proposals and ultimately productive research. The proposal-producing process nevertheless also calls for a complex set of activities and may itself be worthy of evaluation. In this respect, the concept of *process evaluations* (assessments of the interventions alone, and not of any outcomes) arose.

Processes occur over a discrete period of time. Case studies also traditionally trace events over time. Therefore, the case study method was initially conceived as a methodology for doing process evaluations (assessing whether an intervention had been implemented as planned) but not necessarily as useful for doing outcome evaluations. Traditionally, the conduct of a rigorous outcome evaluation was considered as needing unassailable quantitative data not normally accepted as part of a case study.

The concepts espoused in this book are different. Case study evaluations can cover both process and outcomes and can include both quantitative and qualitative data. The case study in this chapter tends to focus on processes (the ultimately important outcomes might be either the proportion of winning proposals or the productivity of the ensuing research). Other cases in this book cover both processes and outcomes.

(For more information, see Yin, 2003, Chapter 5, section on "Explanation Building.")

---

data, to permit later comparisons when FastLane—the electronic system developed by the National Science Foundation (NSF) for submitting proposals, proposal reviews, and grant reports—was to be implemented (the initial implementation was scheduled for 1995-1996). Of the 20 universities in the study, twelve had research administrators who were collaborating in the development of the FastLane system, five participated in the planning of another electronic transmission system being designed by a consortium of other federal agencies, and three participated in both. The study team conducted site visits to 7 of the 20 sites; data from the other 13 were collected through telephone interviews and document reviews. . . .

Data were collected about a university's typical proposal processing, within which three specific NSF proposals and one National Institutes of Health (NIH) proposal also were examined. The research administrators at each university had selected the specific NSF and NIH proposals, with the proposals to vary by discipline, college, and department if possible. All proposals were intended to represent traditional mainstream investigator initiatives, not large institutional competitions, for which funding decisions were reached during academic year 1994-1995. . . .

Within each institution, interview and archival data were collected at four organizational levels: the sponsored research office (SRO) and the college (school), department, and principal investigator (PI) levels. . . . Upon completing the data collection, the team compiled individual databases for each university. Each database contained quantitative and qualitative information on five topics:

1. the specific data collection procedures followed by the research team, for that individual university;
2. proposal submission levels, amount of staff effort, and the electronic (hardware and software) technology available to support the proposal process at the university;
3. the proposal processing and submission procedures for the typical proposal at the university;
4. the anecdotal perceptions and experiences of university personnel and NSF reviewers; and
5. specific administrative tasks related to monitoring proposals and awards (e.g., cash requests and reporting procedures). . . .

Among the research topics, three parameters in the proposal process were given the highest priority: the time needed to process a proposal, the costs involved in that processing, and postsubmission activities. These three were important because the FastLane developers wanted to make sure that FastLane, when implemented, would improve (at least not worsen) these conditions. The following sections analyze the data on the first two of these three parameters.[1] Each section contains its own discussion of research methods, because the data collection varied slightly in investigating each parameter. To ensure confidentiality, dual coding schemes[2] were used in the data tables and flowcharts that appear in this report for each university. . . .

THE TIME NEEDED TO PROCESS AND SUBMIT PROPOSALS

Methodology

To understand the typical proposal preparation and submission process as it occurred during academic year 1994-1995, the study team assembled data for each university that identified (1) the major tasks in the process, (2) the type of task (technical, administrative, or budget related), (3) the level at which the task was conducted (university, college, department, or principal investigator), and (4) the amount of effort required for each task (calendar time and human level of effort). The data were based on interviews about the whole process as well as specific processes that had occurred for the three NSF proposals and one NIH proposal deliberately selected to reflect the typical process within different colleges and departments within the university. The data then became part of the individual databases. From these data, the team developed a flow diagram.

Cross-Case Findings

The 20 universities appeared to follow four different patterns in processing their research proposals:

Group I: The SRO is involved (actively—not just alerting investigators about the opportunity to submit proposals) early in proposal preparation, and the PI submits the final proposal.

Group II: The SRO is involved early, and the SRO submits the proposal.

Group III: All levels are involved early, and the SRO submits the proposal.

Group IV: The departments are involved early, and the SRO submits the proposal.

The groups are arrayed in a hierarchical order, with the lower groups having greater SRO involvement (more centralized) and the higher groups having more departmental involvement (more decentralized).

Figure 9.1 contains the flow diagrams for two contrasting university patterns, one from Group II (University E) and the other from Group IV (University G). In these diagrams, the horizontal axis represents the calendar time taken for the processing (note the scalar distortion), and the vertical axis represents the four organizational levels (from PI to SRO) doing the processing. The University E diagram is more complex than the University G diagram. University E's process also consumes more calendar time. Across all groups, of the original four organizational levels, the college (school) level was found to be the least involved in the process.

The four groups had been defined according to the administrative channels through which proposals flowed. The study now turned to an initially important parameter in proposal preparation—the calendar time needed to process a proposal.

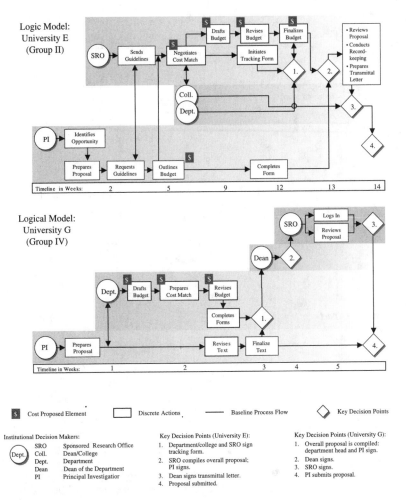

Figure 9.1. Proposal Processing at Two Illustrative Universities

SOURCE: COSMOS Corporation (1996).

The assessment of the time needed to process a proposal did not try to account for the time invested by principal investigators to develop their initial drafts (e.g., in Figure 9.1, the step represented by the "Prepares Proposal" box in the lower-left corner of both illustrations might have consumed any length of time). Rather, the data collection mainly attended to tracking the time consumed by the administrative processes—for instance, reviews, editing, revisions, budget preparation, and sign-offs—once a reasonable draft existed. Furthermore, the study tried to establish

Table 9.1

Proposal Processing Time for Four Groups of Universities

Group Number and Characterization		University Code	Processing Time (Weeks)
Group I: SR0 involved early and PI submits		D	17
	Average Time		17
Group II: SRO involved early and SRO submits		K	14
		E	14
		H	11
		F	10
		N	11
	Average Time		12
Group III: All levels involved early and SRO submits		B	11
		I	10
		O	7
		Q	9
		J	6
	Average Time		9
Group IV: Department involved early and SRO submits		M	5
		P	13
		C	7
		A	5
		G	5
		L	5
	Average Time		7

SOURCE: COSMOS Corporation (1996).

the time needed for the average proposal at a university. Table 9.1 contains the results and shows that when the universities were grouped according to the four groups defined previously, a pattern emerged: Shorter times are associated with universities in the more decentralized groups. . . .

COSTS OF PREPARING PROPOSALS

Methodology

At each university, additional information was collected about the proposal preparation process as it had been experienced during 1994-1995, covering the following categories:

1. the number of proposals submitted;

2. the dollar volume of proposals;

3. proposal budget allocations;

4. total university administrative costs, broken into two components (SRO and department—the latter including schools, colleges, and any other component beneath the SRO),[3] and the proportion of these costs estimated[4] for each component to be for proposal development;

5. the SRO proposal administration staff effort; and

6. the time spent on the proposal process.

Cross-Case Findings

The team focused on calculating two cost indicators: the dollar cost per number of proposals submitted and the dollar cost per dollar value of proposals submitted. To estimate these indicators, the team used two variables as numerators—the total number of proposals and the total dollar volume of proposals submitted. For both indicators, the same denominator was used, derived from the administrative costs associated with the proposal process. Table 9.2 shows the results for each indicator and for each university, with 5 of the 20 universities having insufficient data to calculate the indicators.

A natural assumption, based on a presumed economy-of-scale in dealing with higher volumes of proposals, was that the per-proposal costs would decline as the number of proposals submitted increased. Figure 9.2 tests this assumption by arraying the two variables in a scattergram. However, the scattergram showed just the reverse relationship: Universities with higher volumes of proposals also had higher unit costs (dollars per proposal). The relationship was statistically significant, even given the small number of universities (data points) in the estimate. (To ensure that the extreme outlying data points did not account for this relationship, the figure also shows the correlations when Points A and B are excluded from the analysis.)

Examination of these results on *proposal costs*—along with the earlier results regarding *proposal time* and the four subgroups of universities categorized by their centralized-decentralized hierarchy—showed that the most decentralized arrangements were associated with the higher unit costs, the shorter processing times, but also the higher proposal volumes. The study team offered a tentative explanation for the totality of these relationships, based on the qualitative data that had been collected: The higher unit costs (in the decentralized arrangements) appear to result from having numerous departments participate in the proposal process; at the same time,

Table 9.2

Unit Costs of Proposals, by Number and
Dollar Value of Proposals Submitted, 1994-1995

University Code	Proposal Costs Total (SRO and Department)	Proposal Volume Number Submitted	$ Volume	Unit Cost Per # Proposals	Per $ Million Proposed
A	20,574,176	3,131	1,105,367,674	6,571	18,613
Q	12,870,000	4,250	582,146,000	3,028	22,108
M	5,945,500	3,054	983,874,839	1,947	6,043
N	4,576,300	2,566	105,570,071	1,783	43,348
H	3,957,500	2,028	297,191,823	1,951	13,316
G	3,148,060	1,184	400,071,787	2,659	7,869
F	2,312,900	2,101	402,900,000	1,101	5,741
O	1,933,350	2,224	1,224,004,668	869	1,580
D	1,640,000	3,235	732,636,790	507	2,238
K	947,550	1,277	112,408,806	742	7,741
B	608,476	436	81,341,805	1,396	7,480
J	489,000	1,339	134,176,180	365	3,644
I	200,000	318	44,983,744	629	4,446
T	135,000	635	137,698,881	213	980
P	30,580	96	13,579,628	319	2,252
E	–	2,850	461,639,989	–	–
L	–	2,097	270,107,629	–	–
C	–	2	1,621,418	–	–
R	–	–	–	–	–
S	–	–	–	–	–
Mean	3,957,893	1,824	394,517,874	$1,605	9,827
Median	1,993,350	2,063	283,649,726	$1,101	6,043

Source: COSMOS Corporation (1996).

the expanded participation also means shorter processing times and higher proposal volume across the entire university. The need for numerous departments to participate may reflect more diverse portfolios at the high-proposal-volume universities, including interdepartmental and interdisciplinary proposals. Whether this scenario is correct, or whether mechanical artifacts in the data account for the results, needs to be the subject of future inquiries.

An important caveat to any interpretation based on proposal volume is that the present inquiry made no attempt to examine the eventual award sizes or frequency. The possibility exists that the high-proposal-volume

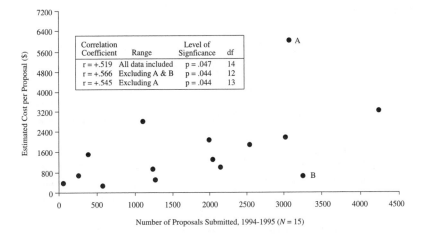

Figure 9.2. Estimated Cost per Proposal, by Number of Proposals Submitted

universities have better "win" rates than the low-proposal-volume univer-sities. If so, the unit costs per award dollar might very well be lower at the high-proposal-volume universities. Such a finding would modify the inter-pretation based solely on unit costs per proposals submitted. Thus this matter also deserves investigation in any further inquiry. . . .

NOTES

1. The original text covering the third parameter has been deleted, to streamline the current chapter.

2. Such a scheme means that a university designated as University A in one table or figure is not necessarily the same university as that designated as University A in another table or figure.

3. Because not all universities were able to provide reliable budget information across all their organizational levels, the data used in the subsequent cost analyses were extracted from a federal data set of university administrative costs compiled annually based on university sub-missions. This data set gives each university's total administrative costs—with breakdowns including the distinction between SRO and departmental costs—to support its indirect rate agreement with the federal government.

4. Whereas the total university costs had been submitted by the universities to the federal government auditors, the estimates of the proportion devoted to proposal development were made by the senior SRO official at each university during interviews for the present study.

10

Case Studies of Transformed Firms

The third and final cross-case analysis returns to a more traditional qualitative analysis. Case studies had been conducted on 14 individual firms.[1] Each had been screened to satisfy two conditions: The firm had to have displayed exemplary bottom-line performance, and there had to be strong evidence that transformation of the entire firm—not just a change in one or a few of its operations—had occurred.

The screening process occurred prior to the actual conduct of the case studies. The subsequent case studies did not entirely corroborate the initial screening. The cases showed that all firms had indeed satisfied the first condition (easier for a screening process to establish), but several of the firms had not really been transformed (harder for a screening process to establish). The resulting cross-case analysis serendipitously took advantage of the inadvertent outcomes of the screening, in the following way: The original plan was to have a series of direct replications; however, the actual cross-case analysis used the variations in transformation to pursue a design reflecting both direct and theoretical replications (see Box 19).

The individual case studies had tried to explain the transformation process. The purpose of the cross-case analysis was to determine whether the firms shared a more generic, common process. To this extent, the purposes of cross-case analyses bear a strong similarity to the motives underlying cross-case syntheses (see Box 20).

AUTHOR'S NOTE: This cross-case analysis by Robert K. Yin appeared as an appendix to the report, *More Transformed Firms Case Studies*, issued by the U.S. Department of Commerce, National Institute of Standards and Technology (NIST), Gaithersburg, Maryland, May 2000, pp. 109-123. The original work has been lightly edited for readability.

BOX 19

Theoretical Replications

This cross-case analysis of manufacturing firms includes some that were transformed (*direct* replications) and others that had not quite become transformed (*theoretical* replications). Replication logic and its contrast to sampling logic have been discussed earlier (see Box 13). The distinction between direct and theoretical replications, however, was not discussed.

In a direct replication, two or more cases are predicted to follow courses of events similar enough that they repeat or replicate each other's experience—in a conceptual, not literal, sense. For example, in the present chapter, nine of the firms originally deemed to be transformed had evidence of the requisite changes listed in Fig. 10.3; unexpectedly, five additional firms did not meet this criterion. As a result, the analysis of how transformation occurs distinguished between the two groups' experiences. The nine were expected to (directly) replicate similar explanations of how transformation occurs, whereas the other five were expected (theoretically) to produce different explanations.

(For more information, see Yin, 2003, Chapter 2, section on "What Are the Potential Multiple-Case Designs?")

BOX 20

Cross-Case Analyses

Cross-case analyses, such as those demonstrated in these last three chapters, bring together the findings from individual case studies and are the most critical parts of a multiple-case study. The analysis treats each individual case study as if it were an independent study. The technique therefore does not differ from any other research synthesis. If large numbers of case studies are being analyzed, the synthesis can use quantitative techniques common to other research syntheses, including meta-analysis. However, the more common situation has only a small number of case studies, requiring alternative tactics. The assembling of word tables, displaying the data from the individual cases and searching for patterns across them, is one such tactic.

(For more information, see Yin, 2003, Chapter 5, section on "Cross-Case Synthesis.")

WHY STUDY TRANSFORMED FIRMS?

The Staying Power of Transformation

Analytic interest in successfully transformed firms (e.g., Garvin, 1993; Hayes and Pisano, 1994; Kotter; 1995; Pascale, Milleman, and Gioja; 1997; and Raynor, 1992) derives from two motives: (1) that such firms can establish world-class performance levels and exemplary business outcomes and (2) that the firms also can maintain their world-class performance for an extended period of time, even as market, technological, and other conditions change.

Maintaining a competitive posture over time—in the face of changing market and technological conditions—drives interest in transformation, because it calls for an adaptive or learning organization (Garvin, 1993). The desired transformation is intended to convey the expectation that a firm's corporate culture and internal systems have not only changed markedly—that is, from one state to another—but they also have become dynamic and can adapt continually to new conditions (Kotter, 1995).

Case Studies of Transformed Firms

To date, little empirical information has been available on the transformation process. How transformation occurs in small- to medium-sized manufacturing firms was therefore the subject of 14 case studies that the National Institute of Standards and Technology and its Manufacturing Extension Partnership (NIST MEP)[2] commissioned during late 1998 and early 1999. Each case covered the pertinent events and outcomes in a single firm. NIST MEP nominated, screened, and selected these cases from field reports strongly suggesting that each represented an instance of a transformed firm, and each firm was willing to serve as the subject of a case study.

Table 10.1 summarizes the basic characteristics of the 14 case study firms: name, location, year started, size, and major product line. Notably, one of the firms (Texas Nameplate) received the Malcolm Baldrige National Quality Award in 1998, the smallest company ever to win this award. This firm has garnered numerous other awards as well.

The main purposes of the cross-case analysis were (1) to summarize the extent and types of transformation in the individual cases (to aggregate knowledge about what constitutes transformation) and (2) to analyze the driving forces that produced transformation among the firms (to increase knowledge about how other firms might promote or facilitate transformation in the future).

Table 10.1

Fourteen Case Study Firms: Year Started, Number of Employees, and Major Product Line

Firm	Year Started	Number of Employees	Products
Boozer Lumber, Columbia, SC	1946—established	145 (present)	Then: cabinets, windows, and doors Now: roof trusses and wall panels
Breeze-Eastern, Inc., Union, NJ	1926—incorporated under the name Breeze Corp. Early 1980s—purchased by Trans-Technology	173 (end of 1998)	Helicopter rescue hoists, external cargo hooks, and cargo winches
Dowcraft Division of the Dowcraft Corp., Falconer, NY	1934—purchased under the name Jamestown Steel Partition Company 1961—became Dowcraft Corp.	50 (January 1999)	Movable steel walls
Dynagear Oil Pumps, Inc., Maquoketa, IA	Year unknown—Hoof Products established 1995—Dynagear, Inc., purchases Hoof 1997—Hoof name changed to Dynagear Oil Pumps, Inc.	137 (present)	Then: governors, timing devices, and oil pumps Now: oil pumps
Forming Technologies, Inc.,* Michigan	Unknown	70	Stainless steel exhaust systems parts
Grand Rapids Spring and Stamping, Inc., Grand Rapids, MI	1960—incorporated as Grand Rapids Spring and Wire Products, Inc. 1985—purchased by Jim Zawacki and Ted Hohman Date unknown—name changed to Grand Rapids Spring and Stamping, Inc.	160 (1998)	Then: springs and wire cable Now: springs and stampings

(Continued)

147

Table 10.1
(Continued)

Firm	Year Started	Number of Employees	Products
Jacquart Fabric Products, Inc., Ironwood, MI	1958—created as a part-time business	52 (present)	Pet beds and other upholstered products
KARLEE Company, Inc., Garland, TX	1974—established	400 (present)	Sheet metal fabricator
MPI,* main plant in Michigan	Founded approximately 80 years ago 1983—sold to conglomerate 1989—65% interest sold to Japanese companies	Fewer than 500	Auto parts—e.g., axles and control arms
Rheaco, Inc., Grand Prairie, TX	Year unknown—Rheaco established	85 (present)	Full-service machining and metal fabricating
Texas Nameplate Company, Inc., Dallas, TX	1946—established	66 (November 1988)	Metal identification and information labels
UCAR Composites, Inc., Irvine, CA	1988—established	70 (present)	Precision tooling for large composite parts
Venturo Manufacturing, Inc., Cincinnati, OH	Year unknown—Venturo established 1989—Collins Associates, Inc., purchases Venturo	40 (present)	Electric and hydraulic truck-mounted cranes
Williams-Pyro, Inc., Fort Worth, TX	1971—established	30 (present)	Stove-top fire extinguishers and connectors

*Fictitious name to protect confidentiality of information provided by company.

WHAT IS A TRANSFORMED FIRM?

Contrasting Transformation With
(Only) Manufacturing Process Improvements

For manufacturing firms, the transformation process contrasts with technical improvements in the manufacturing process alone (see, for example, Upton, 1995). Such improvements can be significant, involving new capital investments, redesigned shop floors, transitions to just-in-time production processes, new plant facilities, and other important changes.

The result may be a marked increase in productivity and profitability. In fact, technical improvements in small- to medium-sized manufacturing firms have been sufficiently challenging that they were the subject of two earlier sets of case studies that NIST MEP published in May 1997 and November 1998. However, despite their significance, such improvements alone may not necessarily involve a change in the firm's culture or produce the dynamic processes needed to sustain the longer-term competitiveness that characterizes transformed firms.

One major difference between transforming a firm and only making manufacturing process improvements may be the extent to which the changes involve employees in developing or sustaining the firm's infra-structure. Although both situations may involve skills training, transformation calls for a deeper empowerment of employees. Empowerment can occur through co-owning a firm; supporting employees' education beyond manufacturing skills training (e.g., helping them to attain high school equivalency certificates); improving wages, fringe benefit packages, and other working conditions; or sharing a firm's management decision-making (not just manufacturing) processes.

As one example, adoption of *cellular manufacturing* or other reorganizations of employees on the shop floor (often resulting in shared manufacturing decision making and significant productivity gains)—unaccompanied by other changes in human resource policies—still only constitutes improvements in manufacturing processes and does not alone result in transformation. Similarly, implementing improvements in human resource systems without making other structural changes in a firm also would be insufficient for achieving transformation.

Other distinguishing characteristics of transformation occur when changes affect a firm's strategic management, its marketing strategies or arrangements, or its use of new information technology, especially when requiring changes in key managerial procedures or norms. Again, the information technology changes should not be limited to the manufacturing process (e.g., implementing computer numerical control equipment) but should join manufacturing processes with business and management systems. The spirit of transformation, therefore, calls for change in the fundamental organization of the operations of a whole firm and not just its manufacturing process or even a combination of manufacturing and marketing changes, as might occur when product lines change.

The desired transforming changes need not occur all at once. The total package of changes over time, however, should be sufficiently strong and different from previous practices to signal a significant competitive repositioning of the firm. Symptomatically, a firm may reflect such repositioning by acquiring a new name.

Toward an Operational Definition

Central to the case studies and to the present analysis was the definition of transformed firms in operational terms. Through its literature review and consultation with experts, the case study team developed an overall framework and a list of the management, marketing, manufacturing, and business processes and policies that might signal genuine transformation. Figure 10.1 shows this framework, depicted as a logic model of sequential changes assumed to be causally related in a successful transformation process. Item 4 in this figure lists five domains for the transforming events. These events, combined with an unspecified change process (see the empty square inside item 4), are claimed to produce the improved business performance in item 7.

Table 10.2 fills in the empty square by listing the management, manufacturing, and business processes and policies expected to change in the transformation process. To become eligible as a case study, a firm had to demonstrate some change in at least four of the first five domains and to provide evidence of significant change in the sixth domain: business results over the past 5 to 7 years.[3] Furthermore, the business results were expected to be greater than mere improvements: The preferred goal was to demonstrate high performance, defined as productivity in the top 25% of firms within the same competitive market. This greater expectation, however, was not a mandatory requirement for a firm to become eligible as a case study.

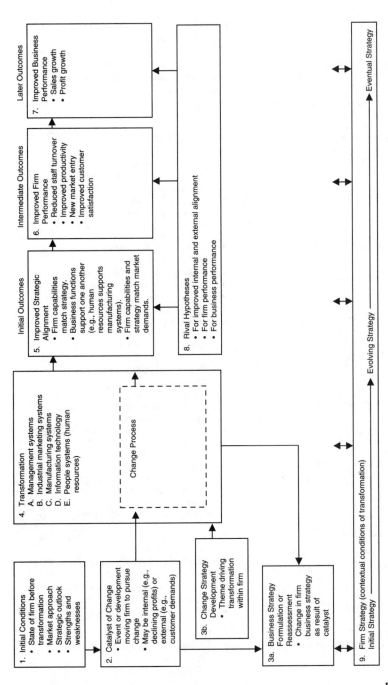

Figure 10.1 Transformed Firms Logic Model

151

Table 10.2

Desired Areas of Changes, for Transformed Firms

The nomination process defined "transformed firms" as firms that have undergone broad-based change, affecting nearly all areas of the business and resulting in real improvements in business performance. Field manufacturing specialists nominated firms on the basis of being able to identify changes in five of the following six categories (the sixth category was mandatory):

Categories of Change	Criteria of Change
Management systems	• Strategic planning processes • Business operations planning processes • Management information analysis and controls • Organizational culture • Financing processes • Administrative services processes
Industrial marketing	• Market competitor analysis • Customer analysis • Product development processes • Sales and territory management • Selling strategies and channel management • Marketing planning process • Advertising and promotion practices
Manufacturing systems	• Product or process design • Facility design • Planning and scheduling process • Procurement practices • Production control processes • Quality assurance processes • Maintenance practices • Environment, health, and safety practices • Distribution practices
Information technology	• Communications infrastructure • Data management practices • Systems implementation • Process analysis and decision support processes • Firm's exposure to the Year 2000 problem
Human resources	• Human resources strategy and management • Job design or analysis • Employee recruitment or selection processes • Compensation and benefits • Employee performance management • Training or employee development practices • Employee relations
Business results (REQUIRED): significant improvement over past 5-7 years	• Customer satisfaction • Productivity (value-added per employee) • Sales • Sales to new customers • Profits

WHAT KIND OF TRANSFORMATION
DID THE FIRMS EXPERIENCE?

Compiling Data From Individual Case Studies

As an initial step, the cross-case analysis called for a careful review of each individual case study. The review attended more closely to the narrative portions of the cases than to the tables that were part of the case presentations (in many instances, the tables were incomplete or inadvertently selective of the information in the narrative). Based on the narratives, the cross-case analysis compiled and organized key information about each firm's assumed transformation, according to the six domains of interest (five organizational domains plus the business results domain).

The original compilation also paid close attention to the calendar year in which the transforming events occurred, addressing two concerns: (1) The compilation represented data on the rapidity or lengthiness of the transformation process for each firm, and (2) the dates provided chronological benchmarks that helped to organize and interpret the causal flow of events, assuming that effects must occur chronologically after causes. Table 10.3 presents highly abbreviated versions of these profiles, to facilitate a view of the entire cross-case pattern across the individual cases.

Application of Operational Definition in the Cross-Case Analysis

Examination of the completed case studies revealed that not all firms in fact turned out to satisfy the needed criteria to be designated as a transformed firm. Such slippage can frequently occur and must always be tolerated in following the current type of case screening process, where eligibility to become a case study depends on alleged organizational processes and not just (business) outcomes. In this design, a thorough and definitive screening process might have required a full case study just as part of the screening process, which is not a feasible expectation. At the same time, those firms that did not fulfill all the original criteria still provided useful information, as discussed next.

Firms Not Quite Transformed

Table 10.3 shows that 5 of the 14 firms were not quite transformed, because they did not show changes in five of the six categories in Table 10.2. In four of the cases (Boozer, Breeze-Eastern, Jacquart, and Venturo), even

Table 10.3

Brief Profiles of 14 Case Studies

Firm Name	Brief Summary of Transformation	Role of CEO in the Transformation Process
Transformed Firms:		
Dowcraft Division	Firm installs new CAD software, revamps sales and marketing network, and creates dynamic strategic plan; establishes ESOP program and starts new training opportunities; implements shop-floor work teams; and completes new manufacturing facility with new manufacturing control system.	President and five employees purchase control of firm. New CEO takes over and presses for changes; WNYTDC helps to define and implement new manufacturing operations.
Dynagear Oil Pumps, Inc.	Firm drops two of three product lines, simultaneously investing in employees' working conditions, pay, and involvement in management; later upgrades information technology (computer systems); changes name of firm; and alters sales arrangements.	Acquisition of firm leads to new CEO, who is driving force for change; IMTC provides some assistance.
Forming Technologies, Inc.*	Firm changes total operation because of shift in basic product material, requiring R&D to solve technical problems; increases employees' pay and benefits, training, and work conditions; and adopts continuous improvement philosophy.	CEO studies needed technical changes (due to shift in customer requirements) and is driving force for all changes.
Grand Rapids Spring and Stamping, Inc.	Firm refocuses product line; installs new manufacturing equipment, including PC access to all employees; reduces number of customers to work more closely with them; and expands employees' involvement in manufacturing and management practices and increases their training.	New owners purchase company, and one serves as new CEO and is driving force for change; MMTC assists in forming minicompanies and continuous improvement.
KARLEE Co., Inc.	Firm initiates leadership teams and strategic planning process, defines new relationships with customers, builds new manufacturing	Spouse of original founder assumes majority ownership and becomes

(Continued)

Table 10.3

(Continued)

Firm Name	Brief Summary of Transformation	Role of CEO in the Transformation Process
	facility with cellular manufacturing, continues to expand facility, and implements new information system integrating business and manufacturing processes.	president and CEO and is committed to building a leadership culture.
MPI*	Firm installs creative manufacturing cells, shifts product focus, improves marketing practices, makes working conditions more equitable, and implements participatory kaizen system.	Internal managers help to get new CEO (who shakes up management ranks) appointed; CEO and new managers are driving forces for change.
Rheaco, Inc.	Firm reorganizes production floor, focuses on smaller number of customers (the profitable ones), installs integrated information system, and invests in employee training and in-house capabilities.	Son of firm's founder becomes CEO, faces production problems. TMAC assists, but CEO is driving force for strategic planning and change.
Texas Nameplate Co., Inc.	Customer's mandated upgrade in production process leads firm to install new equipment, invest in total quality management training, and commit to zero defects; firm also invests in employee programs and completes strategic plan, starts new marketing practices, and upgrades computer system.	Son of owner takes over as president, commits to total quality management and to employees as a company's most important asset. Management sets successively higher standards.
Williams-Pyro, Inc.	Firm streamlines product design, implements cellular manufacturing, installs computerized and automated robotics system; also develops management team and creates participatory climate, along with strategic planning to develop single vision, as well as new marketing initiatives.	New CEO takes over upon death of former CEO, seeks to modernize manufacturing processes; CEO is driving force, but TMAC and senior managers also provide important assistance.

(Continued)

Table 10.3
(Continued)

Firm Name	Brief Summary of Transformation	Role of CEO in the Transformation Process
Not Quite Transformed:		
Boozer Lumber	Firm installs new assembly processes, later constructs new plant; plant workforce declines with combining of two shifts into one; plant productivity and capacity increase; new productivity increases now being sought in marketing area and in firm's other plant.	New person becomes vice president and CEO. SCMEP shares book with CEO, who engages SCMEP to do benchmarking and plan new plant.
	New person becomes vice president and CEO. SCMEP shares book with CEO, who engages SCMEP to do benchmarking and plan new plant.	
Breeze-Eastern	Firm makes manufacturing changes to reduce lead time, production costs, and delinquency rates and to improve inventory turns and cash flow; reorganizes business development staff and marketing strategies; and implements paperless MIS system and performance measurement systems to focus departments on corporate, not just departmental, goals.	New CEO takes over struggling business, downsizes and streamlines operation, and rebuilds management team. Team engages external consultants, working with them for 14 months to clarify business strategy.
Jacquart Fabric Products, Inc.	Firm rearranges production process, changing to just-in-time delivery, using kaizen blitz to engage employees in improved communications, suggestions for new practices, and increased control over management procedures.	Owner (who also was CEO) wanted to improve production process, asked MMTC to assist. It recommended kaizen blitz.
UCAR Composites, Inc.	Firm claims to be constantly transforming, with no settled production process, stable markets, or even permanent location; internal culture retains features of a startup company; major initiatives involve pushing new technologies (production and business	Firm founded 11 years ago is constantly upgrading its machines and computers; parent company supplies funds after requesting that firm develop strategic

(Continued)

Table 10.3
(Continued)

Firm Name	Brief Summary of Transformation	Role of CEO in the Transformation Process
	functions) to their limits; employees typically work long hours and are expected to work better, faster, and cheaper.	plan (had assistance from CMTC).
Venturo Manufacturing, Inc.	Firm installs *kanban* just-in-time system, cutting production cycle time in half and giving employees increased responsibility for the flow of manufacturing; savings in space permit firm to consider strategic investments to grow production capability; new bar code technology now being considered to improve inventory control and production efficiency further.	New parent company purchases firm, relocates it, and streamlines operations. New production coordinator assists plant manager in implementing kanban system, with additional assistance from IAMS.

CMTC: California Manufacturing Technology Center—UCAR Composites
IAMS: Institute of Advanced Manufacturing Sciences, Inc.—Venturo Manufacturing, Breeze-Eastern
IMTC: Iowa Manufacturing Technology Center—Dynagear Oil Pumps
MMTC: Michigan Manufacturing Technology Center—Grand Rapids Spring and Stamping; Jacquart Fabric Products; MPI; Forming Technologies, Inc.
SCMEP: South Carolina Manufacturing Extension Partnership—Boozer Lumber
TMAC: Texas Manufacturing Assistance Center—Rheaco, Williams-Pyro
WNYTDC: Western New York Technology Development Center—Dowcraft
No centers mentioned: KARLEE, Texas Nameplate

* Fictitious name to protect confidentiality of information provided by company.

though the firms had made substantial improvements in their manufacturing processes—including the installation of skills-based training and rearrangements of employees on the shop floor—the apparent transformations were in fact largely limited to these (manufacturing) processes.

Few other major changes, in human resource practices or in significant and broader strategic planning by the firms, were reported, although some changes were still in their planning stages at the time of the case study. For these cases, therefore, transformation may still be occurring, and the firms may meet the transformation criteria at some future date. However, for the present cross-case analysis, these firms were categorized as not quite transformed.

A fifth case (UCAR) was considered different for yet another reason: The firm appears still to be in the entrepreneurial phase of a young firm; for example, the case study suggests that the firm's internal culture still seems to reflect that of a start-up firm. Although the firm was 11 years old at the time of the case study and appeared to be in a continual state of change, the reported changes were not readily distinguishable from the transitions that might have been expected in a new firm during its early years. In this sense, the firm did not appear to have transformed from one state to another. Rather, the firm still seemed to be in its initial phase.

An important reason for distinguishing these five cases from the rest is that any examination of the organizational processes that might underlie transformation should not commingle information from these two groups of cases. In fact, the reverse may be true: The five cases may involve different underlying processes, to be contrasted with the remaining nine firms.

Transformed Firms

These remaining nine cases all did seem to satisfy the criteria for transformation, exhibiting important changes in at least four of the five domains and reporting impressive business results in the sixth domain. Their transformations reflected improvements in their manufacturing operations but also included shifts in organizational practices or norms such as the following:

- *Dowcraft:* Dynamic strategic plan and employee stock ownership program
- *Dynagear:* Open-book management and sharing of financial performance data
- *Forming Technologies:* Continuous improvement, covering broad variety of internal improvements
- *Grand Rapids:* Culture characterized by extensive employee involvement and quest for continuous improvement

- *KARLEE:* Team members taking ownership over corporate objectives
- *MPI:* Creative manufacturing cells
- *Rheaco:* New focus on customer-oriented manufacturing
- *Texas Nameplate:* Continuous improvement
- *Williams-Pyro:* Strategic planning emphasizing a single vision for the firm.

For most of the firms, the transformations appeared to occur over a 5-year period, with Dynagear, MPI, and Williams-Pyro seeming to have accomplished the change in 2 to 3 years.

DID THE TRANSFORMATIONS SHARE COMMON CONDITIONS?

Although the case studies were not intended to analyze the motives for the firms' transformations, the case studies did track some of the conditions underlying the transformation process. On this basis, the cross-case analysis was able to test whether the cases shared a more generic, common process. The analysis found that the nine transformed cases fell into two subgroups.

New Product Lines Can Drive Transformation

In the first subgroup are three firms (Dynagear, Forming Technologies, and Grand Rapids) whose transformations tie directly to substantial changes in either their product lines (Dynagear and Grand Rapids) or raw materials (Forming Technologies, from "mild" steels to stainless steel). In turn, these product-based changes accompanied or required widespread changes in the firms' manufacturing processes, marketing strategies, strategic planning, and relevant technological and human resource support. For Dynagear and Grand Rapids, the product lines changed so much that the firms eventually changed their names, an event not found in any of the other seven cases (though one firm had changed its name well before any transformation process started).

Desire for Productivity Gains Also Can Drive Transformation

In the second subgroup are the other six firms, whose transformation occurred in the absence of major shifts in product lines or materials (although product mixes may have changed). These firms transformed to become more productive, through a broad array of changes in manufacturing processes as well as in the organization of human and technological resources.

Distinguishing these two subgroups is valuable because although many firms may want to make a successful transformation, not all firms will have the opportunity or need to change their product lines or materials substantially. The second group demonstrates that such changes are not necessary to the transformation process. The attractiveness of transformation, in fact, is understanding how to change an existing firm, making it more productive and changing its culture, even when its product lines remain unchanged.

Change in CEO as an Initiating Event

Across both subgroups, the transformation process appeared to emanate from an initial change in CEOs, which occurred in eight of the nine transformed cases (all but Forming Technologies, where the CEO's son drove the change process before buying out his father near the end of the firm's transformation). The CEOs were new for a variety of reasons. Some firms had been acquired by new owners (Dynagear and Grand Rapids). In others, sons had replaced fathers (Rheaco and Texas Nameplate), people had succeeded their spouses (KARLEE and Williams-Pyro), or a succession of CEOs had occurred (Dowcraft and MPI).

The events reported in the case studies suggest that the new CEOs appeared to have had the ambition, talent, and vision to initiate and sustain a transformation process. In the smaller firms, the CEO alone wielded a high degree of influence; in the somewhat larger firms (only two of the nine firms had over 200 employees), the CEO worked with the top managers to influence change.

Among the not-quite-transformed firms, new CEOs or ownership were involved in three of the five cases. Therefore, an interesting possibility is that CEO turnover is a necessary but not sufficient condition for transformation, given the following additional observations.

CEOs' Visions and Subsequent Actions

First, improvements in the manufacturing process and productivity were a clear part of the CEOs' vision. Also important (in seven of the nine cases) was the CEOs' ability to pursue or to put into place a strategic planning or cultural change process that created broad goals for the entire company, such as environmental efficiency, continuous improvement, transition from production-driven to customer-oriented manufacturing, promotion of "business drivers," or development of a rallying theme and philosophy for the firm. In contrast, CEOs or new owners in the not-quite-transformed firms tended to define new needs in less global terms, often relying on a consultant or outside expert to define a more limited technical change.

Second, in eight of the nine cases, the nature of the manufacturing changes or the strategic planning (or both) meant decentralizing control and responsibilities on the shop floor, whether through the creation of manufacturing cells (a frequent change), shop-floor work teams, minicompanies, or employee committees. Such decentralization was not readily evident in the not-quite-transformed firms.

CEOs' Leadership Over External Technical Assistance

Third, another part of the scenario for the transformed firms had to do with the CEOs' use of external technical consultants or assistance. Such assistance occurred with some frequency, in both the transformed and the not-quite-transformed cases.[4]

A possibly subtle difference, however, is that in the transformed cases the CEOs defined and directed such assistance more proactively, whereas in the not-quite-transformed cases the external consultants exerted greater initiative. For instance, in at least four of the five of these latter cases, the consultants appeared to have provided the critical scope and operational definition of the needed changes—for example, a new plant, a SWOT analysis, a *kaizen* blitz training program, and a *kanban* just-in-time manufacturing strategy.

Issues to Be Addressed in the Future

The case studies therefore suggest the beginnings of a common transformation scenario: A new CEO develops a strategic plan or unitary vision, implements improved manufacturing processes that decentralize control to the shop floor, and appears to influence rather than be influenced by external consulting assistance. Possible additions to this scenario, and further details, await more clues to the transformation process. The cases, for instance, did not systematically investigate the possible importance of such processes as MRP systems, ISO 9000 or related registrations, clean plant and other environmental initiatives, employee incentive systems, turnover in other key personnel, or changes in other personnel or managerial policies. These topics require further investigation.

The evolving general scenario does suggest that a key ingredient for transforming a firm may be turnover in the CEO position rather than the transformation of an incumbent. The cross-case evidence also suggests that transformed firms may not be significantly different from "turnaround" or "turnover" firms. Whether this observation is true of most transformed firms also remains to be tested in future cases.

At the same time, the possibly critical vision and commitment of the CEO raises an important policy question for NIST MEP in offering technical assistance to firms: How can one know beforehand if a new or incumbent CEO is capable and willing to lead a transformation process? Likewise, how might NIST MEP or other consultants effectively engage and convince a CEO to undertake and lead a transformation process?

SUMMARY: GENERAL LESSONS ABOUT TRANSFORMED FIRMS

The current set of case studies has illustrated the transformation process, distinguishing it from other, more traditional technical improvements in manufacturing processes. Empirical evidence, based on a serendipitous cross-case design comparing nine of the firms with the other five (see Box 21), suggests the following conclusions.

Transformed firms have successfully made broad changes across their whole enterprise, thereby producing marked and discontinuous improvement in their business performance. Furthermore, transformation can be accomplished with or without major changes in a firm's product lines or basic product materials, although such changes could drive the transformation process.

Nine of the 14 cases met the criteria for transformation, the other five being considered not quite transformed. The nine transformed firms had accomplished their transformations over roughly a 5-year period. Two of these nine seemed to have completed the change in 2 to 3 years.

The typical scenario for transformation, derived from the nine cases, started with a change in the firm's CEO, followed by actions reflecting the ambition, talent, and vision of the new CEO. Such actions included important technical improvements in the manufacturing process but also put into place strategic planning, cultural change, or related processes.

BOX 21

Logical Positivism

All of the chapters in this book have shown how case studies can be conducted through the collection and analysis of empirical data. Findings and conclusions are then derived from these data. *Logical positivism* is the philosophical school of thought that espouses this practice, which is the foundation for the natural sciences.

Traditionally, case studies have not always been considered to be a method in the logical positivist tradition. Instead, some believe that case studies also can be done where an investigator's intuition and ideas—not reinforced by the objective collection of empirical data—have prevailed. An entirely different way of developing conclusions, apart from the scientific method, is the result. However, the present book and its companion textbook (Yin, 2003) do not subscribe to such an approach. Our approach has been to place case study research within the framework of the scientific method—to develop hypotheses, collect empirical data, and develop conclusions based on such data. The result is not claimed to be science but the emulation of the scientific method.

(For more information, see Yin, 2003, Chapter 1, section on "The Case Study as a Research Strategy.")

Transformation also included decentralizing control and increasing responsibilities to the shop floor, if not throughout the entire firm. As noted, this scenario was not as readily identifiable in the five not-quite-transformed cases. Although those cases underwent substantial improvements in the manufacturing process—which included redesign of shop floors, implementation of just-in-time procedures, or installation of new technologies—these improvements alone did not translate into a strategic vision or decentralized control.

NOTES

1. Chapter 6 of this book presents one of the individual case studies. The case studies involved field-based inquiries—with consultants or other experts making site visits to the firms—to analyze the firms' records, examine documents and related materials, interview key

people, and observe manufacturing and business processes. Different consultants and experts participated, each authoring different case studies. Despite this diversity, all authors participated in an initial and intensive training workshop, shared a similar orientation toward the underlying conceptual framework, and agreed to follow similar case study and evidentiary procedures. As a result, the individual case studies reflected a series of parallel inquiries.

2. The individual case studies and the cross-case analysis were part of a project conducted by COSMOS Corporation for NIST MEP, whose mission is to strengthen the global competitiveness of U.S.-based, small- to medium-sized manufacturing firms.

3. The original pool of nominees came from consultants and staff associated with NIST MEP Centers. The nominated firms, however, did not need to have had any prior affiliation or relationship with a NIST MEP Center.

4. In many instances, the external assistance had been provided by NIST MEP's manufacturing extension centers, although the cases were not selected because of this assistance.

References

Academy for Educational Development (AED). (1995). *Technical assistance briefing book for community planning groups.* Washington, DC: Author.

Bickman, Leonard. (1987). The functions of program theory. In L. Bickman (Ed.), *Using program theory in evaluation: New directions for program evaluation* (pp. 5-18). San Francisco: Jossey-Bass.

Centers for Disease Control and Prevention. (1998, February). *External review of FY98 HIV prevention cooperative agreement applications: Summary of process and findings.* Atlanta, GA: Author.

Chen, Huey-tsyh. (1990). *Theory-driven evaluations.* Newbury Park, CA: Sage.

Chen, Huey-tsyh, & Rossi, Peter H. (1989). Issues in the theory-driven perspective. *Evaluation and Program Planning, 12*(4), 299-306.

COSMOS Corporation. (1985, December). *Attracting high-technology firms to local areas: Lessons from nine high-technology and industrial parks.* Bethesda, MD: Author.

COSMOS Corporation. (1986, September). *Managing for excellence in urban high schools: District and school roles.* Bethesda, MD: Author.

COSMOS Corporation. (1989, September). *Interorganizational partnerships in local job creation and job training efforts: Six case studies.* Bethesda, MD: Author.

COSMOS Corporation. (1996, November). *The National Science Foundations FastLane System baseline data collection: Cross case report.* Bethesda, MD: Author.

COSMOS Corporation. (1999, July). *Final report for the evaluation of the CDC-supported technical assistance network for community planning,* Vol. I. Bethesda, MD: Author.

COSMOS Corporation. (2001, March). *National evaluation of the local law enforcement block grant program: Final report for Phase I.* Bethesda, MD: Author.

Downs, George W., Jr., & Mohr, Lawrence. (1976, December). Conceptual issues in the study of innovation. *Administrative Science Quarterly, 21,* 700-714.

Garvin, D. A. (1993, July-August). Building a learning organization. *Harvard Business Review,* 78-91.

Ginsburg, Alan L. (1989, December). Revitalizing program evaluation: The U.S. Department of Education experience. *Evaluation Review, 13,* 579-597.

Glaser, Barney G., & Strauss, Anselm L. (1967). *The discovery of grounded theory: Strategies for qualitative research.* Chicago: Aldine.

Gries, David. (1987, February). Final grant report for National Science Foundation Award No. DCR81-05763 to Cornell University.

Hayes, R. H., & Pisano, G. P. (1994, January-February). Beyond world class: The new manufacturing strategy. *Harvard Business Review,* 77-86.

Kotter, J. P. (1995, March-April). Leading change: Why transformation efforts fail. *Harvard Business Review,* 59-67.

Mohr, Lawrence. (1978, July). Process theory and variance theory in innovation research. In Michael Radnor et al. (Eds.), *The diffusion of innovations: An assessment.* Evanston, IL: Northwestern University.

National Commission on Neighborhoods. (1979, March). *People, building neighborhoods.* Washington, DC: U.S. Government Printing Office.

National Institute of Standards and Technology (NIST). (1999, April). *Transformed firms case studies.* Gaithersburg, MD: U.S. Department of Commerce, NIST.

Ogawa, Rodney T., & Malen, Betty. (1991, Fall). Towards rigor in reviews of multivocal literatures: Applying the exploratory case study method. *Review of Educational Research, 61,* 265-286.

Pascale, R., Milleman, M., & Gioja, L. (1997, December). Changing the way we change. *Harvard Business Review,* 127-139.

Pyecha, John N., et al. (1988). *A case study of the application of noncategorical special education in two states.* Research Triangle Park, NC: Research Triangle Institute. (Robert K. Yin collaborated in the design, conduct, and analysis of the research.)

Raynor, B. (1992, May-June). Trial-by-fire transformation: An interview with Globe Metallurgical's Arden C. Sims. *Harvard Business Review,* 117-129.

Trochim, William M. K. (1989). Outcome pattern matching and program theory. *Evaluation and Program Planning, 12*(4), 355-366.

Upton, D. M. (1995, July-August). What really makes factories flexible. *Harvard Business Review,* 74-84.

U.S. General Accounting Office (GAO). (1987, April/1991). *Case study evaluations.* Washington, DC: U.S. GAO, Program Evaluation and Methodology Division.

Wholey, J. (1979). *Evaluation: Performance and promise.* Washington, DC: The Urban Institute.

Yin, Robert K. (1981a, September). The case study as a serious research strategy. *Knowledge: Creation, Diffusion, Utilization, 3,* 97-114.

Yin, Robert K. (1981b, March). The case study crisis: Some answers. *Administrative Science Quarterly, 26,* 58-65.

Yin, Robert K. (1981c, January/February). Life histories of innovations: How new practices become routinized. *Public Administration Review, 41,* 21-28.

Yin, Robert K. (1991, Fall). Advancing rigorous methodologies: A review of "Towards rigor in reviews of multivocal literatures," *Review of Educational Research, 61,* 299-305.

Yin, Robert K. (1982, September/October). Studying phenomenon and context across sites. *American Behavioral Scientist, 26,* 84-100.

Yin, Robert K. (1984/1989/1994). *Case study research: Design and methods.* Newbury Park, CA: Sage.

Yin, Robert K. (1992). The role of theory in doing case studies. In Huey-tsyh Chen & Peter H. Rossi (Eds.), *Using theory to improve program and policy evaluations* (pp. 97-114). Westport, CT: Greenwood Publishing.

Yin, Robert K. (2000). Cross-case analysis of transformed firms. In *More transformed firms case studies* (pp. 109-123). Gaithersburg, MD: U.S. Department of Commerce, National Institute of Standards and Technology.

Yin, Robert K. (2003). *Case study research: Design and methods* (3rd ed.). Thousand Oaks, CA: Sage.

Yin, Robert K., & Gwaltney, Margaret K. (1981, June). Knowledge utilization as a networking process. *Knowledge: Creation, Diffusion, Utilization, 2,* 555-580.

Yin, Robert K., & Moore, Gwendolyn B. (1988, Fall). Lessons on the utilization of research from nine case experiences in the natural hazards field. *Knowledge in Society: The International Journal of Knowledge Transfer, 1,* 25-44.

Yin, Robert K., & White, J. Lynne. (1985). Microcomputer implementation in schools: Findings from twelve case studies. In Milton Chen & William Paisley (Eds.), *Children and microcomputers: Research on the newest medium* (pp. 109-128). Beverly Hills, CA: Sage.

Yin, Robert K., et al. (1979). *Changing urban bureaucracies: How new practices become routinized.* Lexington, MA: Lexington Books.

Index

About the Author

Robert K. Yin is President of COSMOS Corporation, an applied research and social science firm. Over the years, COSMOS has successfully completed hundreds of projects for federal agencies, state and local agencies, and private foundations. Within the firm, Dr. Yin still directs individual projects, including those using the case study method. Most of the applications reported in this book derive from work done with COSMOS's projects. The firm is located in the Washington, D.C., metropolitan area (Bethesda, MD) and has been in operation since 1980.

Dr. Yin has authored numerous other books and articles. His first book on the case study method, *Case Study Research: Design and Methods,* has had three editions (1984, eight printings; 1989, eleven printings; and 1994, thirteen printings). He is a member of the Cosmos Club and has served as Visiting Scholar to the U.S. General Accounting Office. Dr. Yin received has B.A. in history from Harvard College (magna cum laude) and his Ph.D. in brain and cognitive sciences from M.I.T.

APPLIED SOCIAL RESEARCH
METHODS SERIES
Series Editors
LEONARD BICKMAN, Peabody College, Vanderbilt University, Nashville
DEBRA J. ROG, Vanderbilt University, Washington, DC

Other volumes in this series are listed on the series page.